湖南省2012年教学与改革项目课题成果（课题编号G21209）
湖南科技大学规划教材
中南大学出版社规划教材项目

# 乒乓球

## 汉英双语教程（第二版）

何阳 ◇ 编著

*Chinese-English Bilingual Course*
*on Table Tennis*

中南大学出版社
www.csupress.com.cn

·长沙·

# 编委名单

编　著：何　阳
副主编：李忆湘
编委会：陈　瑶　　陈水波　　郭清林　　黄衣慧
　　　　李立志　　刘头生　　彭丽红　　李协吉
　　　　谭　亮　　王雪峰　　唐祥彬　　吴　聪
　　　　边　惠　　张　扬　　王　琳

# 前　言

　　现今对专业课程使用外语进行"双语教学"已成为我国各高等学校学科课程教学改革的热点和发展趋势，乒乓球学科是我国各高等体育院校的主干课程之一。鉴于我国乒乓球运动处于世界的领先地位，对乒乓球课运用"双语教学"有着积极的、重大的现实意义。随着我国职业乒乓球运动的不断发展和国外运动员的积极加入，以及对外输出乒乓球人才的需要，我国对既掌握乒乓球专业技能又懂乒乓球专业英语的高素质人才的需求大增。故此，只有掌握了乒乓球专业英语才有可能承担起交流、展示和传播我国先进的乒乓球文化精髓的任务，才有可能更好地推动国际乒乓球运动事业的可持续发展。《乒乓球汉英双语教程》应运而生，本教程着眼于为新世纪培养国际化体育双语人才，从我国体育学院学生英语水平的实际出发，经多次双语教学实验改进编写而成，旨在提高我国高等体育院校学生乒乓球技术水平的同时提高其专业英语水平，为培养国际化的乒乓球体育人才打下坚实基础。

　　《乒乓球汉英双语教程》编写思路有别于国内许多现已出版的体育术科类双语教材，不是简单地将原版的外文教材全盘翻译过来，更不是英译汉的双语教程，而是鉴于我国乒乓球运动在世界的领先地位，依据我国体育学院学生英语水平的实际情况，在大量阅读乒乓球原版教材的基础上筛选材料，结合我国高等体育学院乒乓球教材的知识体系，仔细研究，精心编写的以汉语为主、英语为辅的双语教程。其主要特色：一是知识体系完备、双语突出，结构层次清楚。全书以我国高等体育院校乒乓球教材的基本知识体系为主，重在将乒乓球运动的基本技术用汉英双语编写，突出动作方法与动作结构要点，同时也强调双语的教学与实践，如第六章课堂双语教学用语，则按英汉来编写，强调英语的运用。二是表达明确，简单易学。全书以汉语表达为主、英语表达为辅，力求易学易记，灵活运用。三是图文并茂，生动形象。代表性的技术动作均配以图示，专业术语全部从英文原版教材中筛选。本教程主要适用于体育学院乒乓球普修、专（选）修等本科生、研究生或高、中等学校体育乒乓球选修课程；也可作为将要援外的乒乓球教练员、运动员的培训教材以及对乒乓球运动专业英语感兴趣的人士。

　　《乒乓球汉英双语教程》为2012年湖南省教学改革的课题成果，历时两年教学试验，主要针对高等体院乒乓球双语教学的实际需要，突出专项特点，并吸收国外原版教材中最新教学方法和理念，结合国内教材的知识体系，努力做到使本教程具有时代的新特点和专业课教材的特色。同时，解决目前高等体育院校乒乓球双语教学无完整知识体系教材的现状，促进高校乒乓球课程教学改革的深入及教学质量的提高，为其他运动技术课程进行双语教学提供可借鉴的思路与途径。

第二版的编写着重补充了关于裁判员临场操作与竞赛编排以及乒乓球专业词汇中的裁判用语。乒乓球裁判员在比赛过程中的操作，对比赛的顺利进行起着重要作用，所以，提高乒乓球裁判员的技能，增强临场情绪的控制与调节，对乒乓球比赛的顺利进行有着重要的意义。乒乓球竞赛的组织与编排，书中说明了竞赛项目和基本比赛方法，可指导大家合理地从事乒乓球训练，以达到保持健康和提高运动竞技水平的目的，并进一步地帮助学生学习与巩固乒乓球运动的基本知识。

《乒乓球汉英双语教程》一书由何阳副教授编著，李忆湘教授担任副主编，各章节中文部分负责人分工如下：李立志(湖南科技大学教育学院研究生)负责第一章的编写工作；郭清林、王雪峰(湖南科技大学体育学院讲师)负责第二章的编写工作；刘头生、陈水波(湖南科技大学体育学院研究生)、陈瑶(湖南科技大学教育学院研究生)负责第三章的编写工作；黄衣慧(中南林业科技大学体育学院讲师)、李协吉(湖南科技大学体育学院讲师)负责第四章的编写工作；李忆湘(湖南科技大学体育学院教授)、彭丽红(湖南科技大学教育学院研究生)、谭亮(江西师范大学体育学院研究生)负责第五章的编写工作；何阳负责第六章的编写工作；吴聪(国际级乒乓球裁判)、张扬(湖南第一师范学院讲师)、边惠(湖南科技大学教育学院研究生)、王琳(湖南科技大学体育学院研究生)、负责第七章的编写工作。全书由何阳副教授负责汉英翻译、统编定稿。在编写过程中，我们主要参考了刘建和的《乒乓球教学与训练》，苏丕仁的《现代乒乓球运动教学与训练》，王吉生的《乒乓球拍探秘》，全国体育院校教材委员会审定的《乒乓球》，魏中明的《汉英体育词汇大全》，蔡继玲、吴修文等的《跟专家练乒乓球》等书籍。在此，真诚地向上述作者深表谢意！同时感谢湖南科技大学体育学院体教系乒乓球专选班易俏(2010级)、谭栖(2010级)、张配雯(2011级)、张凯丽(2012级)等同学在此书的资料整理、编辑、出版过程中付出的辛勤努力。

由于水平有限，书中的疏漏及错误之处在所难免，我们衷心地欢迎广大读者对本书提出宝贵意见。

作者　何阳
2017 年 01 月

# 修订版说明

  本教程自 2014 年秋季在湖南科技大学等省内六所体育院校试用以来，得到了广大师生的一致好评。随着乒乓球运动的不断发展，结合各校教学实践中反馈的意见，我们对教程进行了一次集中的修订。此次修订主要增加了第七章竞赛组织与裁判技能方面的知识，同时补充了部分专业英语词汇、增加了全英文专业词汇注解和修正了部分小错误，其中全英文专业词汇注解可供更高层次专业人士学习。

  在此衷心感谢对本教程提出宝贵意见的教师与学生。

作者　何阳

**2018 年 3 月 18 日**

# 目　录

# Contents

# 第一章　乒乓球运动发展概况
## （The development of table tennis）

## 一、乒乓球运动的起源（Origin of table tennis）

乒乓球起源于 19 世纪末的英国，是由网球运动派生出来，并命名为"桌上网球"（table tennis）。当时，乒乓球运动作为游戏，成为家庭娱乐活动的流行项目之一。大约在 1890 年，有位名叫詹姆斯·吉布（James Gibb）的英格兰人到美国旅行时，偶然发现了一种用赛璐珞制成的空心玩具球，弹跳力很强。于是，他对这种球稍加改进后用于该游戏，之后"桌上网球"逐步在英国和世界各地推广起来。因为此球在桌上打来打去发出"乒乒乓乓"的声音，英国一家体育用品公司，首先用"乒乓"（Ping Pong）一词作了广告上的名称。就这样，乒乓球才开始得此绘声之名。1926 年 1 月，在德国柏林举行了一次国际乒乓球赛，同年 12 月，国际乒乓球联合会正式成立，简称国际乒联（International Table Tennis Federation，ITTF），并把在伦敦举行的欧洲锦标赛命名为第 1 届世界乒乓球锦标赛（World Table Tennis Championships，WTTC）。

## 二、乒乓球运动发展简况（Brief introduction to the development of table tennis）

乒乓球运动的发展史，从某种意义上讲，是在球拍（bat）工具不断革新，使球在速度（speed）和旋转（spin）之间相互竞争过程中向前推进的。从 1926 年第 1 届世界乒乓球锦标赛到现在，乒乓球运动发展经历了以下几个时期。

## （一）欧洲乒乓球运动全盛时期（Table tennis heyday in Europe）（1926—1951 年）

首先，在这25年间，共举行了18届比赛，各届举办地点先后为：英国、瑞典、匈牙利、德国、匈牙利、捷克斯洛伐克、奥地利、法国、英国、匈牙利、奥地利、英国、埃及、法国、英国、瑞典、匈牙利和奥地利。仅第13届比赛在非洲的埃及举行，其余17届皆在欧洲举行。其次，在7个正式比赛项目中，先后共有117个冠军［第11届女单（women's singles）无冠军，故为118减1］。除美国选手取得8个冠军外，其余都由欧洲选手获得，占全部锦标赛冠军的93.1%。再次，参加比赛的国家也主要是欧洲的。基于以上三个原因，故此称为乒乓球在欧洲的全盛时期。在技术打法上，虽然第1届的男子单打冠军雅可比和前5届的女子单打冠军梅德尼扬斯基都是左右开弓（smash from both wings）的进攻型打法，但其后的世界冠军都是以削为主（chop play）或削攻结合型打法（chop and attack play）。所以，就总体而言，这一时期的主导打法是削球，指导思想为"自己少失误，让对方失误"。

## （二）日本称雄世界乒坛时期（The period dominated by Japanese table tennis）（1952—1959 年）

日本乒协早在1928年就加入国际乒联（ITTF），但直到1952年才第一次参加世乒赛。日本选手手握海绵球拍、采用直拍全攻型打法，结合快速的步法移动，击败了欧洲的下旋削球（under-spin chop），从此使上旋打法占了优势。他们连续击败了许多欧洲防守名将，一鸣惊人地获得了男子单打（men's singles）、男子双打（men's doubles）、女子团体和女子双打（women's doubles）四项锦标赛的冠军。从此，世界乒乓球技术的优势开始由欧洲的削球（chop）转向了亚洲的攻球（attack）。进攻与防守成为当时世界乒乓球技术的两种打法。此时期共举行了7届世乒赛（19～25届），共有锦标赛冠军49个，日本队独拿24个冠军，占全部锦标赛冠军的49%。特别是1954年的第21届世乒赛，日本队获男、女团体冠军；在1959年的第25届世乒赛时，日本队竟然拿走了7项冠军中的6项，此时期日本当之无愧称雄世界乒坛。

### （三）中国乒乓球运动的兴起（The rise of Chinese table tennis movement）（1961—1969 年）

20 世纪 50 年代末，正当日本队处于巅峰状态时，中国选手容国团在第 25 届世乒赛上，为中国夺得了第一个世界冠军。1961—1969 年，共举行 5 届世乒赛。中国队仅参加了第 26、27 和 28 届的比赛，3 届共计 21 个锦标赛冠军，中国选手获得了 11 个冠军，占全部锦标赛冠军的 52%。第 29 和第 30 届世乒赛中国队未能参加，但从当时的技术实力分析，中国队还是占上风的。具有"快、准、狠、变"（speed，accuracy，aggressiveness and variation）独特风格的中国近台快攻打法和以"稳、低、转、攻"（stability，low，spin and attack）为指导思想的中国削球打法，把世界乒乓球运动推向了一个新的发展阶段。20 世纪 60 年代初，日本运动员创造了一种新技术——弧圈球（loop）。由于它当时还处于初级阶段，虽然旋转强烈，但弧线高、速度慢，所以，未能充分显示出应有的威力。不过，弧圈球对以后世界乒乓球技术的发展却起到了很大的促进作用。

### （四）欧洲乒乓球运动的复兴与欧亚争夺（The renaissance of European table tennis movement and the Eurasian race）（1971—1987 年）

进入 20 世纪 70 年代，世界乒乓球技术的发展突飞猛进。欧洲选手经过了近 20 年的努力，兼取中国快攻和日本弧圈球打法的优点，创造了弧圈结合快攻和快攻结合弧圈的两种新打法，从而走上复兴之路。欧洲选手自从走上速度与旋转结合之路后，就显示出了旺盛的生命力，但因在技术上还存在着某些漏洞，一直未能有根本性的突破。直到 20 世纪 80 年代末期，欧洲队以弧圈球结合快攻形成了全方位进攻型打法（attacking play），台内、近台、中远台球能攻，正手、反手、侧身能攻，下旋、上旋能攻，低球、高球能攻。与此同时，我国的近台快攻打法和直板快攻结合弧圈球打法也有一定的提高和发展，在一系列的国际比赛中，战胜了不少著名的欧洲选手，取得了良好的成绩，形成了以中国队为首的亚洲队同欧洲队争霸的局面。

### （五）进入奥运时代，欧亚竞争更加激烈，中国渐显霸主地位（Entering the Olympic era，Eurasian competition is more intense，but China has supremacy）（1988—1999 年）

1988 年，乒乓球成为奥林匹克运动会正式比赛项目，这大大推动了世界乒乓球运动进一步发展。这时期欧洲队把弧圈球与快攻结合，把过去速度与旋转的绝对对抗，演变成速度与旋转的对立统一，从技术动作到打法类型无不体现了这一新理念。他们的进攻范围更广，具备了全方位进攻的实力。20 世纪 80 年代末至 90 年代中期，中国男队走入困境，女队遭遇困扰。标志乒乓球技术最高水平的男团（men's team）、男单（men's singles）冠军，连续 3 届（第 40、41、42 届世乒赛）为欧洲选手所获。然而在 1995 年第 43 届世乒赛上中国包揽 7 个冠军；1996 年亚特兰大奥运会上中国包揽所有冠军；1997 年第 44 届世乒赛上中国仅丢失男单一个锦标赛冠军，这无疑向世界证明了中国乒乓球再上辉煌征程，让世界再次迎接中国乒乓球的全盛时期。

## （六）新世纪新规则，中国勇于创新，一枝独秀（Although there is a series of new rules in the new century, China outshines others with bold innovation in match）（2000 至今）

自 20 世纪末始，国际乒联对乒乓球进行了一系列改革，这些改革虽不会改变乒乓球运动最基本的规律，但对技术、战术的影响还是不容忽视的：通过减弱发球的威胁性，使比赛在更公平的条件下进行，更多地进入中局；通过降低击球速度，降低旋转强度而增多了击球的回合数量，使广大观众再一次品到了乒乓球的魅力。在实施新赛制的 4 届奥运会比赛中，中国选手仅丢失一枚金牌；女子乒乓球世界杯从 1996 年开办，所有冠军被中国女子乒乓球队包揽，连续两届（第 50 届、51 届）世乒赛的 5 个正式比赛项目的决赛全部在中国选手之间进行。从欧亚对抗到中国的全盛，世界乒坛的格局不但没有均衡发展，反而更加集中，中国选手的优势也更加明显，世界乒坛正处于中国一枝独秀的时期。

# 三、乒乓球运动的发展趋势（Development trend of table tennis）

根据乒乓球的发展规律，我们可以预见，各种打法会不断地完善和充实，技术将更加精益求精，乒乓球规则和器材的变革推动着新的先进技术的产生。随着更多新技术的不断出现，仅靠某个技术称雄世界已是不可能的事情。当今以及未来一段时间内乒乓球运动发展的趋势是：技术全面、特长突出、积极主动、凶狠快速、勇于创新。

第一，现代乒乓球运动比赛集中表现为强相持（sustained rally）、强对抗（confront stroke）、旋转（spin）强、力量（force）重、速度（speed）快、落点

（placement）刁，运动员只有技术全面才有可能组合多种技术，灵活运用，达到制敌效果。

第二，高水平运动员必须拥有最独特的乒乓球技艺，助其在前三板（first three strokes）过程中占据主动，赢得先机（如张继科的全台反手拧球发球技术）。

第三，乒乓球运动一定要强调意识上的主动，谁主动谁就占得抢攻的先机，接发球（receive）直接抢攻将成为争取主动的前沿技术，技术组合更加细腻、战术运用更加合理。

第四，技术打法向凶狠快速方向发展是总趋势中的一个重要方面，速度和旋转互相渗透，力量与技巧互相融合，强调凶狠、速度的优势和有效性，要想取胜，就必须快速上手，打出快速有力的快攻或结合快速旋转的弧圈快攻。

第五，不管团体或个人，只有在技术全面的基础上不断创新，才有可能领先于世界，常盛不衰。因此，勇于创新也是未来乒乓球发展的一个方向。在运动员技战术发展的同时，我们必须加强对运动员心理素质的培养，提高运动员的心理承受能力，培养勇于挑战、永不服输的坚定毅力和气势。

总体而言，世界乒乓球运动将朝着以上5个方面发展。通过2013年第52届世界乒乓球锦标赛可以看出，中国男子运动员将"快、准、狠、变、转"（speed，accuracy，aggressiveness，variation、spin）的技术风格发挥得淋漓尽致，向着更快、更狠、更新的方向发展，这也是世界乒乓球运动技术的发展方向。

# 第二章　乒乓球基本理论知识
# （Basic theories of table tennis）

## 一、乒乓球运动设备（Table tennis equipment）

### （一）常用乒乓球运动设备（Table tennis equipment in common use）

选择乒乓球设备时，应检查该设备是否在国际乒联备案以及被批准，上面是否具有 ITTF 的标志。这些设备主要包括：场地、球桌、球网、球、底板、胶皮、胶水、发球机等。

**1. 场地（playing area）**

规范的乒乓球场地在大小、灯光、地面等方面都有具体要求。

（1）面积（area）。赛区应由 0.75 m 高的同一深色的挡板（barrier）围起，并与相邻的赛区及观众隔开，每张球台的比赛场地面积为不少于 14 m 长 ×7 m 宽（轮椅运动员比赛项目面积不少于 8 m×6 m），室内垂直高度不得低于 5 m。每张球台至少要使用两台电子计分牌，决赛时使用四台。电子记分牌（electronic scoreboard）安放在乒乓球比赛场地两侧的后面或四角，使观众在看台上可以清楚地看到显示屏上的比分。体育馆内还有一个所有观众都能看清楚的大电子显示屏（electronic display），能同时显示所有球台比赛的有关信息。

（2）灯光（light）。奥运会为了保证电视转播影像清晰，要求照明度为 1500～2500 Lx（勒克斯，光照度的单位），所有球台的照明度是一样的。如果需要增加临时光源，该光源从天花板上方照下来的角度应大于 75°。比赛区域其他地方的照明度不得低于比赛台面照明度的 1/2，光源距离地面不得少于 5 m。场地四周一般应为深颜色，观众席上的照明度应明显低于比赛区域的照明度，要避免耀眼光源和未遮蔽窗户的自然光。

（3）地面（floor）。地面应为木制或经国际乒联批准的品牌和种类且可移动塑胶地板。地板具有弹性，没有其他体育项目的标线和标识。地板的颜色不能太浅或反光强烈，可为红色或深红色，不能过量使用油或蜡，以避免打滑。

### 2. 球桌(table)

球桌有一条白色的边线(side line)和端线(end line)以及中线(center line)。宽为1525 mm，长为2740 mm，高(台面距地面)为760 mm，球网高152.5 mm，球网长为1525 mm(台宽) + 152.5 ×2 mm。

### 3. 球网(net)

球网装置包括球网、悬网绳、网柱(pole)及将它们固定在球台上的夹钳部分。球网应悬挂在一根绳子(cord)上，绳子两端系在高152.5 mm的直立网柱上，网柱外缘离开边线外缘的距离为152.5 mm。整个球网的顶端距离比赛台面152.5 mm。整个球网的底边应尽量贴近比赛台面，其两端应尽量贴近网柱。台面四边涂上20 mm宽的白线，台面中间应有一条3 mm宽、与球台长边平行的中线。

### 4. 球(ball)

国际乒联在2000年对比赛用球做出了一项重大改革，球的直径从38 mm增至40 mm，更改的原因是为了使球能在屏幕上看得更清楚。比赛用球颜色必须是白色或橙色且标有由ITTF批准的3星高质量球，1星和2星球则为质量较差的球，一般为练习和娱乐用球。所有经ITTF批准的标准用球都要经过圆度(roundness)、硬度(hardness)和反弹性(inverse elasticity)的标准检测。

### 5. 底板(blade)

乒乓球底板至少应有85%的天然木料。加强底板的黏合层可用各种纤维材料(如碳素纤维、玻璃纤维等)，每层黏合层不超过底板总厚度的7.5%或0.35 mm。拍头(racket head)在大小上有些差别，防守球员经常使用柄头尺寸略大的球拍。大多数底板制作商是根据速度来制作底板的，一般来说，击球速度越快的球拍，其控球的能力较差。底板的类型多种多样，大多数底板重80～90 g，选择底板一般是以手柄(handle)握在手中的舒适度来决定的。最受欢迎的手柄类型有FL手柄、ST手柄和AN手柄。

### 6. 胶皮(rubber)

现有的胶皮种类繁多，因而使得乒乓球与其他的球拍类运动相比，乒乓球运动有着更多种类的打法。乒乓球套胶由胶皮和海绵（sponge）组成，但胶皮和海绵的总厚度不能超过 4 mm，在官方比赛中使用的球拍两面的颜色必须是一黑一红。

一般来说，胶皮表面有五种类型：正胶（短颗粒胶）（short pimps rubber）、长胶（长颗粒胶）（long pimps rubber）、防弧胶（anti-spin rubber）、生胶（rubber）、反胶（inverted rubber）。正胶海绵拍的反弹力好，回球速度快，能制造一定的旋转，但不如反胶转；长胶胶皮拍的胶粒高度为 1.6 ~ 2 mm，主要依靠旋转强或冲力大的来球增加回球的旋转强度，来球旋转弱或冲力小，回球旋转也弱，它比普通的胶皮拍难于控制，击球速度也不快；防弧胶海绵拍的海绵特别软，弹性差，可以削弱旋转球的作用，便于控制对方的弧圈球；生胶海绵拍的反弹力强，回球速度快，摩擦力较小，造旋能力差；反胶海绵拍的胶皮表面平整，有较大的黏性，摩擦系数大，能击出强烈的旋转球，但反弹力稍差，回球速度不如正胶海绵拍。

### 7. 胶水（glue）

过去乒乓球专用胶水中起作用的有两部分——黏合胶体和有机溶剂。黏合胶体是起黏合作用的，如海绵和底板、胶皮和海绵的黏合，而起到快干胶水决定性作用的是有机溶剂，这里的有机溶剂是指低毒性的、有挥发性的、能溶解黏合胶体的化学溶剂。2008 年 9 月 1 日起，国际乒联要求运动员只能使用更环保、健康、绿色的无机胶水。有机胶水（organic glue）与无机胶水（inorganic glue）的最大区别在于是否含有有毒化学成分，有机胶水气味刺鼻，无机胶水却没有。

### 8. 发球机（table tennis robot）

发球机能够有效地帮助球员进行实践训练。它的发球可以根据需求改变旋转、速度和落点，从而让练习者可以在很短时间内获得最大限度的训练，主要用于初学者（beginner）和需要提高运动强度（exercise intensity）的运动员。发球机的主要功能包括以下 5 点：

（1）可发上、下、左、右旋球，以及各种侧上、侧下混合旋球，采用双轮驱动，因而速度旋转都分别可调，同时亦可发不转球。

（2）可上下调整出球的俯仰角度，任意设置前后或左右落点变化，实现定点、多区域以及全台多点发射。

（3）出球速度（speed）、频率（frequency）、机头摆动速度均设多档，可任意调整。

（4）含自动回收和供球系统，持续击打，无须捡球。

（5）快速安装与拆卸，只需几分钟，无须任何工具。

## （二）乒乓球拍配置方法（Methods of choosing table tennis rackets）

《论语》曰："工欲善其事，必先利其器。"乒乓球运动的"神兵利器"自然是挥洒在人们手中的球拍。对于热爱乒乓球运动的人们来说，乒乓球拍在他们心中有不可言喻的地位。那么，究竟怎样选择适合自己的球拍呢？总的来说包括两个原则。

### 1. 要与自己的打法适合（bats should match the play）

什么打法选什么球拍。球拍的性能要与使用者击球风格相匹配。"击球风格"指的是人们在运用相同的击球技术时表现出不同的心理趋向——或快、或变、或凶、或稳。就运动员的打法风格来说，追求凶狠打法的人喜欢快速的球拍，追求多变打法的人喜欢"持球"时间长的球拍。这就是球拍与打法的统一，因此在专业使用的底板拍面上，多标明有"进攻"（attack）、"全面"（allround）、"防守"（defend）等类型的分类表示。人们可以根据自己追求的风格来选择球拍，一般来讲，一个通用的原则就是，在保证自己满意的球感的条件下，尽量选稍微弹一些的球拍。比如，一个人击球球感很好，击球技巧也运用得很好，但是击球的杀伤力不是很足，所以可以选择弹性更大的球拍以加强自己的速度，提高杀伤力（lethality）来维持较高技术水平的发挥。（见表2-1）

表2-1 技术打法与底板搭配表

| 打法类型 | 主要击球范围 | 主要击球方式 | 底板选择建议 | | | | | |
|---|---|---|---|---|---|---|---|---|
| | | | 纯木底板（层） | 纤维底板 | 单面贴重量（g） | 双面贴重量（g） | 厚度（mm） | 球感 |
| 近台快攻 | 近台 | 弹、打推、拉扣 | 5~7 | 碳素、玻纤、芳基 | 90~95 | 85~90 | 6以上 | 较硬 |
| 快攻弧圈结合 | 中、近台 | 推、打冲、拉扣 | 5~7 | 碳素、玻纤、芳基碳素混织 | 90~95 | 85~90 | 5.5~6 | 柔中弹 |
| 快速弧圈攻击 | 中、远台 | 拉、冲 | 5或独木 | 芳基、玻纤、芳基碳素混织 | 85~90 | 80~85 | 5.5~6.5 | 柔中弹 |
| 攻守结合 | 中、远台 | 搓、削拉、攻 | 5~7 | 芳基玻纤 | — | 80~90 | 6左右 | 软弹 |
| 少儿初学者 | 近台 | 推、搓攻、拉 | 5~7 | 不限 | 80~85 | 75~85 | 6左右 | 柔和 |

**2. 球拍与海绵和胶皮的平衡（the balance of the bottom slab，sponge and rubber）**

软硬互补是"统一与平衡"的搭配原则，球拍的底板（blade）、海绵（sponge）、胶皮（rubber）搭配须追求"统一与平衡"。弧圈球打法使用容易制造旋转（spin）并离台击球有速度的高弹力底板与较硬海绵的反胶球拍；近台快攻选手选择反弹速度更快的硬底板与软海绵的正胶球拍；削球选手选择易于控球（ball control）、变化（change）和接弧圈球的大板面底板与薄海绵的长胶球拍。这都是追求打法与球拍底板、海绵、胶皮的统一。

当打法基本确定之后，球拍的选择搭配应该依据以强为主、追求平衡、软硬互补、重在掌握的原则。所谓以强为主，是首先考虑打法中首选技术特点对球拍性能的要求，在满足技术强项的前提下，兼顾其他技术对球拍性能的要求；追求平衡的原则要求选择球拍时应该尽可能做到突出特点、兼顾全面，也就是说，不应让使用者在运用某项常用技术时有明显的不适应感；软硬互补是球拍匹配追求平衡的一般原则；重在掌握的原则指的是球拍匹配追求的最终目标，匹配得当的球拍能够帮助运动员驾驭所有运用的技术，不应追求一个方面的极端特色而在另一方面失去对击球的控制。

举两个例子说明。一是弧圈球打法，通常是使用高弹力的软底板，可以通过底板的自身形变提供较强的旋转和离台后的速度，通常使用硬海绵和软胶皮搭配，在这种组合下可以打出既有旋转又有速度的弧圈球；二是快攻打法，近台快攻选手可以选用硬底板与较软的海绵搭配，这样可以使球提高脱板速度和反弹速度，更容易体现正胶近台快攻的节奏速度。当然，如果近台快攻选择反胶也是可以的，但是注意所选择的海绵也应该比弧圈球打法的稍微软一些才好。

按照如上的搭配原则，我们可以总结出两种常用的平衡搭配法（见表 2-2）：

（1）弧圈球打法的配置：

软底板（soft blade）＋ 硬海绵（hard sponge）＋ 软反胶皮（soft inverted rubber）。

（2）近台快攻打法的配置：

硬底板（hard blade）＋ 软海绵（soft sponge）＋ 硬正胶皮（hard short pimps rubber）或硬反胶皮（hard inverted rubber）。

表 2 - 2　技术打法与海绵、胶皮搭配表

| 打法类型 | 主要攻球特点 | 胶皮选择建议 | | 海绵选择建议 | |
|---|---|---|---|---|---|
| | | | | 厚度(mm) | 硬度(HS) |
| 近台快攻 | 弹、打、推挡、拉、扣 | 正胶 | 大颗粒 | 2.0 以上 | 38 |
| | | 反胶 | 高弹力 | 2.0 以上 | 42～46 |
| | | 生胶 | 大颗粒 | 2.0 以上 | 40 以下 |
| | | 长胶 | 硬质 | 0.5～1.0 | — |
| 快攻弧圈结合 | 推、打、冲拉、扣 | 反胶 | 高弹力—高黏性 | 2.1 以上 | 44 以上 |
| | | 生胶 | 大颗粒 | 1.8 以上 | 40 以下 |
| 快速弧圈结合 | 拉、冲 | 反胶 | 高黏性—高弹性 | 2.1 以上 | 46 以上 |
| 攻守结合 | 搓、削拉、攻 | 反胶 | 高黏性 | 2.0 以上 | 40～46 |
| | | 长胶 | 软质—硬质 | 0.5 左右 | — |
| | | 正胶或生胶 | 小颗粒—大颗粒 | 0.5 左右 | — |
| | | 防弧胶皮 | 软质—硬质 | 1.5～2.0 | 30 以下 |
| 少儿初学者 | 搓、推攻、拉 | 反胶 | 高黏性—高弹性 | 1.9～2.1 | 42～46 |

## 二、乒乓球比赛常用规则(The common rules of table tennis matches)

乒乓球比赛是 11 分制，获胜者必须净胜两分，也就是说获胜者是先于对手达到 11 分并领先 2 分。如果双方同时达到 10 分，则继续比赛，直至一方领先 2 分为获胜者。比赛的局数为奇数，如三局两胜(the best of 3 games)、五局三胜(the best of 5 games)、七局五胜(the best of 7 games)，其中后两者较为常用。在决胜局中，一方先得 5 分时，双方应交换方位(change ends)。

在竞技比赛中，裁判员一般以掷硬币或猜边的方式来决定选择发球或者选边的一方。如该运动员选择发球，则在下一局比赛开始时，由另一方发球。在比赛中采用双方轮流发球的规则，在一方发球两次后换发球方，当双方比分达到 10:10 时，则采用每人发一球后就换发球的规则直至比赛结束。

在以下情况中可得分：对手发球失误；对手接球失误(有三种情况：一是对手未能接到来球；二是对手接来球后未能把球送到你这边的桌面；三是当来球

在对方桌面跳两次前，对手未能接到球）；对手的非持拍手（free hand）接触了台面。

当发球者在发球，非持拍手抛球时，只要球离开手掌，则为有效球。在此过程中有以下几点要求：发球必须发在球台水平面以上，也就是说不能在台下抛球；发球必须在球桌端线之后及不能在台内发球；不能用身体的任何部位遮掩击球瞬间，以免阻挡对方视线；抛出的球要接近垂直且至少要有约16 cm 高，并且只能在球的下降期击球；击球后球的第一落点必须在发球者这方的半台内，在飞过球网后，第二落点必须在对方半台上，发球时擦网，应重发球（let）；若不能同时满足以上要求则视为发球违例。

在双打比赛中，当确定发球方后，发球方有权决定第一个球的发球者，而对方队员也有权决定第一个接球者。两分球以后，前两球的接球者成为发球者，而前两球的发球者以外的另一名同队队员则变成接球者，再次两分球后交换发球方，规则同上并以此类推。与此同时，无论是哪方发球，发球者必须在右半台（中线以右）发球，使得球的第一落点在本方的右半台（right half court），第二落点必须在接球方的右半台。

## 三、乒乓球运动的基本术语（Basic terms of table tennis）

### （一）球台（Table）

（1）台面（playing surface）：球台的上层表面称为"台面"。台面长2740 mm，宽1525 mm，离地面高度760 mm。

（2）端线（end line）：台面两端长1525 mm，宽20 mm 的白线称为"端线"。

（3）边线（side line）：台面两端长2740 mm，宽20 mm 的白线称为"边线"。

（4）中线（center line）：台面正中、与边线平行的，宽2 mm 的白线称为"中线"。

（5）台区（court）：台面被平行于端线的球网分开，划为两个大小相等的"台区"。（如图 2 - 1 所示）

### （二）击球范围（Range）

（1）半台（half-court）：中线将每个台区分为左、右两个"半台"（其左右方位依击球方而定）。半台又称"1/2 台"。

（2）1/3 台：台区左侧 1/3 部分称为"左 1/3 台"；台区右侧 1/3 的部分称为"右 1/3 台"。

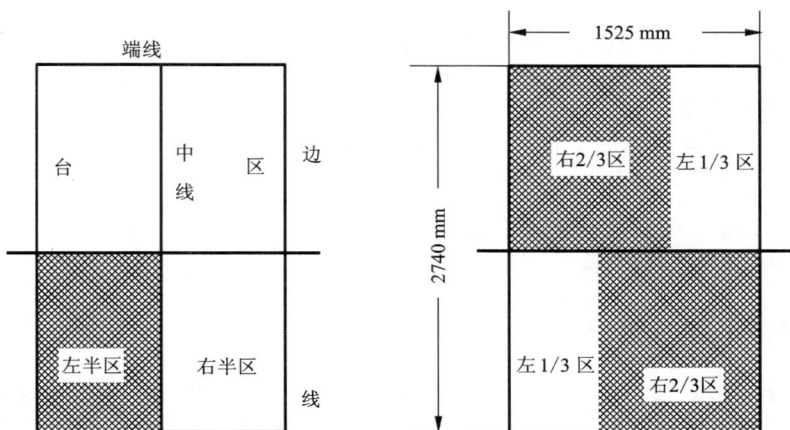

**图 2 - 1  球台**

（3）2/3台：台区左侧2/3部分称为"左2/3台"；台区右侧2/3的部分称为
"右2/3台"。

## （三）站位（Stance）

运动员站立的位置叫站位。根据运动员所站立的位置与球台端线之间的距
离，可将站位划分为：

（1）近台（close to table）：距离端线50 cm以内的范围。

（2）中台（middle ground）：距离端线70 ~ 100 cm处。

（3）远台（far from the table）：距离端线150 cm以外的范围。

（4）中近台：介于中台与近台之间。

（5）中远台：介于中台与远台之间。（如图2 - 2所示）

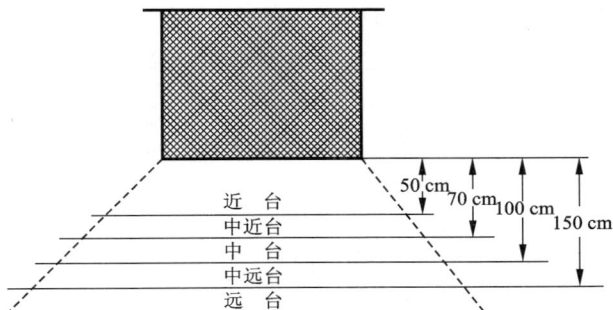

**图 2 - 2  站位**

## (四)击球点(Hitting point)

击球点是指击球时,球拍与球体相接触的那一点的空间位置。击球点的位置是相对击球者身体而确定的,主要包含三个方面的内容:

(1)击球点相对身体的前后位置。

(2)击球点相对身体的左右位置。

(3)击球点相对身体的高低位置。

## (五)击球时机(Hitting timing)

击球时机是指击球时球拍接触的瞬间,球体在空间所处的时期。来球从着台点反弹跳起至回落到地面的整个过程,可分为上升、高点、下降三个时期(如图2-3所示)。

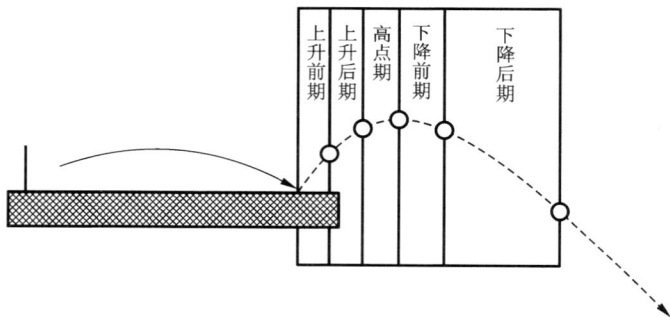

图2-3 击球时机

(1)上升期(rising stage):来球从台面弹起到接近最高点这段过程称为"上升期"。上升期又可分为上升前期和上升后期。

上升前期:指来球从台面弹起后上升的最初一段。

上升后期:指球继续上升至高点期的一段。

(2)高点期(peak stage):弹起的球处于最高点或接近最高点这段过程称为"高点期"。

(3)下降期(falling stage):球从高点期回落至地面这段过程称为"下降期"。下降又可分为下降前期和下降后期。

下降前期:指球从高点期回落下降的最初一段。

下降后期:指继续下降至地面的一段。

## （六）击球部位（Striking spot on the ball）

击球部位是指触球瞬间球拍击在球体上的位置。击球部位的划分，可以击球员为准，先将一个球分为4个面，即：前面（很少击球至此面，只在偶尔遇到对方打的回头球时，击球者随球跑过网，才会击球至此面）；后面（最常见的击球面）；左侧面（如侧身正手发高抛抖动式发球时，多触球在此面）；右侧面（如正手发奔球时，多触球在此面）。击球通常划分为中部（at center）、中上部（above center）、中下部（below center）。（如图 2 – 4 所示）

## （七）触拍部位（Contact spot on the racket）

触拍部位是指击球瞬间，球体触及在球拍上面的位置。一个球拍可分为拍柄、拍肩、拍身三个部分，拍身又可分为拍面和拍身边缘。球拍的击球拍面又可划分为左、右、上、下、中等部位。（如图 2 – 5 所示）

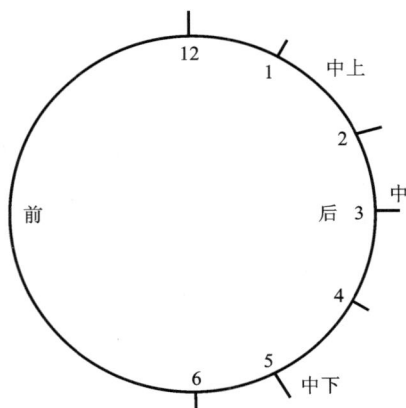

图 2 – 4　击球部位

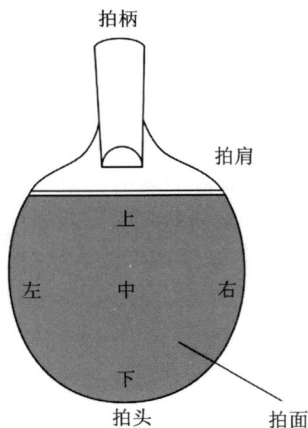

图 2 – 5　触拍部位

## （八）拍形（Angle and direction of racket）

拍形是指击球时拍面所处的角度和方向（angle and direction）。

（1）拍面角度：击球时，击球拍面与水平面所形成的夹角（以拍面的下沿与水平面相交）叫"拍面角度"。拍面角度大于 90°时，称为"拍面后仰"（racket tilted backward）。击球时的拍面角度，按其击球部位的不同可以分为：（如图 2 – 6所示）

拍面向下——击球的上部；拍面前倾——击球的上中部；拍面稍前倾——击球的中上部；拍面垂直——击球的中部；拍面后仰——击球的下中部；拍面稍后仰——击球的中下部；拍面向上——击球的下部。

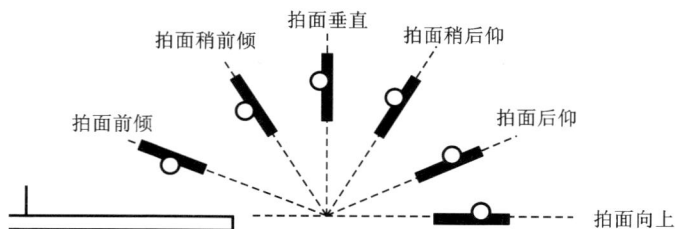

图2-6 拍面角度

（2）拍面方向：击球时，击球拍面所朝向的方位叫"拍面方向"。拍面方向的确定以击球者为基准，拍面向左时击球的右侧，拍面向右时击球的左侧。一般情况下，球拍击球正后方的情况实际上并不多。在多数情况下，不是偏左，就是偏右。因此，要依靠调节拍面来掌握击球动作。

（3）拍面横度：指球拍绕前后轴转动而形成的拍面角度的变化。拍柄与球台端线垂直时为0°，随球拍绕前后轴不断向左转动而增加其左横角度。当拍柄与球台端线平行时，为左横90°；球拍绕前后轴向右转至与球台端线平行时，为右横90°。平常说的拍形呈半横状，即是横度为45°之意。（如图2-7所示）

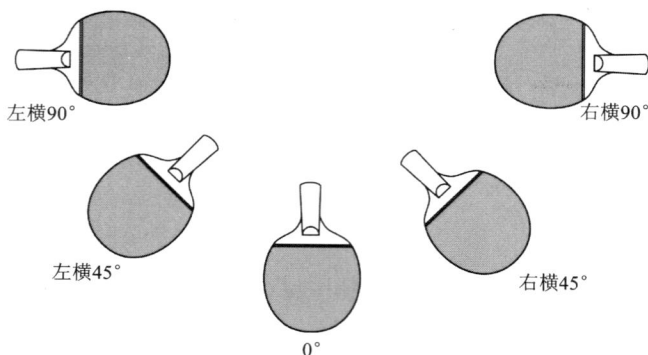

图2-7 拍面横度

## (九)击球路线(Path of stroke)

击球点与落点之间连线的投影线叫"击球路线"。在乒乓球台上,有五条基本击球路线,即右方斜线、右方直线、左方斜线、左方直线和中路直线。击球线路的方位依击球者而定,以右手执拍为例:右方斜线、直线即正手斜线、直线;左方斜线、直线即反手斜线、直线。(如图 2 – 8 所示)

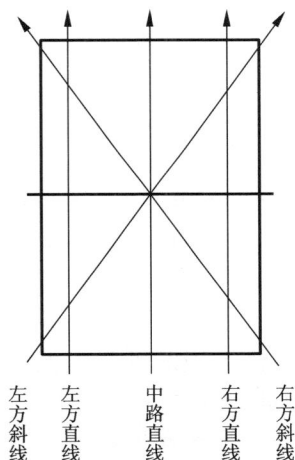

| | | | | |
|---|---|---|---|---|
| 左方斜线 | 左方直线 | 中路直线 | 右方直线 | 右方斜线 |

图 2 – 8 击球路线

图 2 – 9 短球与长球的落点

## (十)短球、长球与追身球(Short serve, deep serve and body hit)

(1)短球(short serve):落点在近网区内(距球网 40 cm 以内),且反弹跳起后的第二落点不超越端线的球。

(2)长球(deep serve):落点在底线区内(距端线 30 cm 以内)的球。

(3)追身球(body hit):击向回球者身体位置(主要是胸腹部位,使回球者不能保持适宜的引拍空间)的球。(如图 2 – 9 所示)

## (十一)击球距离(Length of stroke)

挥拍击球时,球拍的起始点(即引拍结束时的球拍位置)到击球点之间的挥拍长度,称为"击球距离"。(如图 2 – 10 所示)

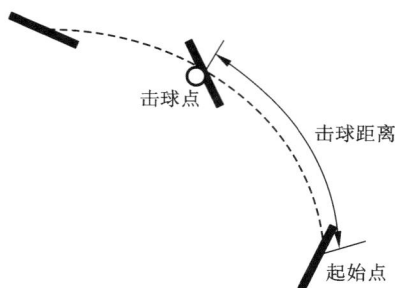

图 2-10 击球距离

## （十二）直拍握拍法（Pen-hold grip）

直拍握拍法的基本动作是：球拍柄右侧贴在食指的第三关节处，以食指的第二关节压住球拍的右肩，食指的第一关节自然向内弯曲，拇指的第一关节压住球拍的左肩（拇指与食指之间的距离要适中）。其他三指自然弯曲斜重叠，以中指第一指节托于球拍背面，使球拍保持平稳。

根据每个运动员打法的不同又有很多微调，快攻型的可基本保持上述握法；两面攻（反手攻）运动员应适当将拍柄靠近食指的第二、三关节之间，以拇指和食指的第一关节压住球拍的左右两肩，拇指和食指距离可比基本动作略小；弧圈类打法，中国式直拍与基本动作类似，但是日式直拍则不同，日式直握法应拇指贴在球拍左侧，食指轻轻扣住拍柄，形成一个小环状，中指和无名指较直地以第一指节托住球拍背部，小指自然紧贴在无名指之下；直拍削球型的握拍是拇指自然弯曲，紧贴拍柄左侧，第一指节用力下压，其余四指自然分开托住球拍背面。（如图 2-11 所示）

直拍握拍法的优点是手腕动作灵活，发球变化多，拍形变化快而灵活，有利于正、反手击球动作迅速转换，有利于处理台内球、追身球。缺点在于照顾范围小，反手攻球受身体限制不易发力，回接弧圈球尤为突出。

图 2-11 直拍削球握法

## (十三)横拍握拍法(Hand-shake grip)

通常横握球拍有两种基本握法。(如图2－12所示)

(1)浅握(shallow grip):以中指、无名指、小指自然地握住拍柄,拇指在球拍的正面轻贴在中指旁边,食指自然伸直斜放于球拍的背面,虎口轻微贴拍。

图2－12　横拍握拍法

(2)深握(deep grip):它与浅握的握法基本相同,不同之处在于虎口须紧贴球拍。

这两种握法,正手攻球时食指要用点力,也可将食指往上移动一些帮助压拍;反手攻球或快拨时,拇指要用点力,也可用拇指往上移动一些帮助压拍。正、反手削球时,手指基本不动。

横拍握拍法的优点是照顾范围较大,击球时便于发力,削球旋转力比直拍强。反手攻球动作小,速度快,攻削交替运用,握法变动不大,利于攻守结合的发展。缺点在于正反手交替击球时,左右摆速不如直拍快,发球时手腕动作不如直拍灵活,处理台内短球、追身球较困难。

## 四、乒乓球竞技制胜因素(Winning factors of table tennis matches)

乒乓球运动是我国的传统优势项目,在世界乒坛保持着长盛不衰的局面。这种成功的实践过程与中国对乒乓球项目的制胜因素、制胜规律的正确认识过程紧密相关。而乒乓球的制胜因素是从经验中积累的,其中有五个物理的竞技要素,是在经验上抽象而成的概念,是对乒乓球运动的本质认识。(如图2－13所示)

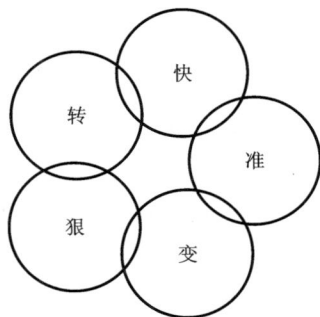

图2－13　乒乓球竞技的制胜因素

## （一）快（Speed）

乒乓球当中的"快"指的是球速，球速具有使对手任何合理的技术动作遭到一时破坏的杀伤力。乒乓球运动在快速多变中，想要加强自身的击球速度，就要学会短时间击球，加快挥拍击球的速率。从理论上来分析，想要加快击球的速度，一方面是尽可能地缩短合理还击所耗费的时间，另一方面是尽可能地缩短球在空中飞行的时间，这将是最理想的。以下几方面可用来参考提高击球速度：

（1）站位靠近球台，在来球的上升期击球。这不仅缩短了击球的时间，而且缩短了回球的飞行路线，同时还借助于来球的反弹力加快回球的速度。

（2）在允许的范围内，尽量压低球的弧线，减小落点的距离，使回球的弧线得以缩短。

（3）还击时，充分发挥击球力量，使击球点尽量靠近球的球心，这样的力量是最大的，加快球的回击速度。

（4）不断提高反应速度和移位速度，这样就有足够的时间等待回击的时间，使之与击球速度紧密配合。

## （二）转（Spin）

旋转极其强烈的球同样也是具有杀伤力的。旋转是制胜的核心因素，有着重大的作用，在旋转中，并不是越转越好，而是旋转的变化越多越好，但又必须明确加转是基础和前提，没有加转，旋转就会失去意义。想主动发力而使球有强烈的旋转就要有好的手感，而良好的手感还是要靠平时多练习搓功、拉球等技术。

因为在乒乓球中，旋转也有不同的效果，如何增强球的旋转，以下几方面是我们应该认识的：

（1）击球时球拍给球的作用力远离球心，保持较长的力臂，即球拍给球的侧方用力大于正方用力。

（2）摩擦球时，必须加快挥臂速度（handwave speed），把力量集中在击球上。

（3）适当利用对方来球的速度，合理借力。

（4）利用向内的摆动弧线摩擦击球（friction contact），可使球拍与球之间的摩擦时间增长，从而使摩擦的效果增强。

## （三）准（Accuracy）

所谓的"准"就是回击球时到对方球台的落点要准，弧线适中。研究球的落点和击球路线，对于提高击球效果和战术应用是十分关键的。落点的运用，主要有：

（1）扩大对方的移动范围（moving range）。

（2）增加对方让位的难度。

（3）紧逼对方的弱点（weakness）和压制对方特长（strong point）技术的发挥。

（4）攻击对方判断与移动的相反方向。

制造不同的弧线曲度，主要根据三个条件：

（1）拍形角度（racket angle）。后仰越大，击球部位应降低；反之，拍形越前倾，击球部位应升高。

（2）击球的部位。击球时以摩擦球为主，减少向前还击力量，可以缩短打出的距离。

（3）发力方向。击球时力量通过球心，向前还击力量越大，摩擦越小，打出距离就越长。球打出距离相同的条件下，发力方向越向上，所产生的球的弧线曲度则越大；若发力方向向前或向前下方，球的弧线曲度则减小。

## （四）狠（Aggressiveness）

"狠"主要体现在力量上，击球力量的大小主要取决于击球时挥拍时的加速度，所以击球时要收紧小臂，使自己有更大的爆发力。从力学原理的角度看，力量＝质量×加速度。力量的大小取决于击球质量的大小和加速度的快慢。增强击球力量的主要方法有：

（1）击球前身体略向前移，使击球点与身体的距离稍远一些，保持球拍与来球有一定的挥拍距离，以利于加大击球的速度，增大击球点力量。

（2）击球前手臂肌肉一定要放松（relax），在击球的一瞬间加力挥拍，使球的速度加快。

（3）击球时，应使身体协调配合，并将力量集中在击球的一瞬间，这样既增加了外力给予球的力量，又配合提高了挥臂动作的加速度。

（4）适当增加球拍的重量及弹性，有利于增加击球的力量。

## （五）变（Variation）

"变"包括了两个方面的内容：主动变化、灵活应变。

（1）主动变化（take initiative to change）：若仅凭单一的战术运用，极易被对手察觉，很难奏效。只有准备行动时意图的虚实真假之"变"，才能创造有利时机，达到攻其不备、出奇制胜的目的。

（2）灵活应变（play to the score）：运动员丰富的比赛经验是应变的关键，准确的观察判断是灵活应变的基础。交锋中运动员战术变化就是围绕着预见性和随机性展开的。

在比赛对抗中，双方运动员的制约，最终就是通过击球的弧线、速度、旋转、力量、落点这5个物理要素来实现的。"快、转、准、狠、变"这5个制胜因素是提高乒乓球运动水平高低的过程。这5个因素构成了乒乓球的制胜因素"群"，"群"中的各因素并非单独存在，各因素之间存在着一定的关系和组合方式，如"快"与"狠"、"快"与"转"、"快"与"准"、"快"与"变"、"狠"与"准"、"狠"与"变"、"准"与"变"等。必须处理好这些关系，才有望在对抗中取得胜利。总而言之，乒乓球运动的发展本质就是这五个制胜因素在相互作用、相互联系、相互影响中不断前行。

# 五、击球动作结构（Structural elements of stroke）

乒乓球的技术动作多种多样，方法各有不同，但在击球动作结构方面却有着共同的规律。一般分为：击球前选位、引拍、挥拍击球、顺势挥拍（跟随）、还原5个部分。

（1）选位（ready position）：根据来球的线路和落点，合理、迅速地移动到适宜的击球位置。

（2）引拍（backswing）：迎球挥拍前的准备动作，为的是更好地发力击球。引拍的方向决定着回球的旋转性质，引拍是否及时决定着能否击打合适的击球点。

（3）击球（contact）：从引拍后的位置挥动到击中来球这段过程。挥拍方向也决定着回球的旋转性质和回球的路线。挥拍（swing racket）弧度大小和加速度的快慢，决定着球的飞行速度、旋转强度和力量。击球部位与拍面角度相互对应，结合挥拍方向来完成回球时采用的技术动作，是决定回球方向、落点（placement）、力量、旋转的关键。

（4）顺势挥拍（跟随）（follow-through）：指击球后由于惯性而随势前挥的一段动作。这样能够保证击球动作的稳定和完整，有利于击球动作的准确性。

（5）还原（recovery）：一个技术动作结束后，以最近的路线、最快的速度回到原来的准备姿势。包括上肢手臂、躯体和下肢的还原。

另外需要注意的是，在完成某一击球动作时，持拍手（racket hand）上臂

（upper arm）、前臂（forearm）和手腕（wrist）的发力主次与腰（waist）、腿（leg）及非持拍手等需全身配合协调发力。

　　作为一名教师或教练员，除了要很好地掌握乒乓球击球动作结构的共同规律外，还要了解所有技术动作结构（structural technical actions）的单个特点，对这些特点进行讲解和示范。这样才能提高教学的系统性，按照动作结构去观察学生、运动员的动作，发现其动作的错误所在，抓住关键进行纠正，加快学生和运动员掌握正确的技术动作。故此，了解击球动作结构，对提高分析技术动作的能力和教学训练的质量是有很大帮助的。

# 第三章　乒乓球基本技术
# （Table tennis basic techniques）

## 一、基本站位和预备姿势（Basic stance and ready position）

乒乓球运动员的基本站位，应该根据不同类型打法及个人打法特点来决定，这样才会有利于技术特长的发挥。不同类型打法的运动员有几种基本站位：左推右攻打法（backhand block with forehand attack）运动员的基本站位在近台中间偏左；两面攻打法（attack on both sides）运动员的基本站位在近台中间；弧圈球（loop）打法运动员的基本站位在中台偏左；横板攻削结合打法（combination of attack and chop）运动员的基本站位在中台附近；以削（chop）为主打法运动员的基本站位在中远台附近。

运动员在回击每一个来球之前，应当使身体保持正确的基本姿势，以便迅速启动，抢占合理的击球位置（getting good stroke position），然后才能及时正确地把球回击过去。

正确的基本姿势应该是：两脚平行站立（略比肩宽）、提踵、前脚掌内侧用力着地，两膝微屈、上体略前倾；重心置于两脚之间；下颌稍向后收，两眼注视来球。以右手握拍为例，持拍手臂自然弯曲置于身体右侧，手腕放松持拍于腹前，身体离台 20～30 cm。总结为"注视来球、上体微倾、屈膝提踵、重心居中"。

两脚开立略比肩宽，是为了保持身体重心的稳定性；两膝微屈、脚内侧用力着地，有利于迅速蹬地起动；提踵的动作对保证快速启动具有重要作用。

## 二、发球技术（Serve）

在乒乓球技术中，发球（serving）是唯一不受对方来球控制的技术。它具有极强的主动性，可以选择自己最适合的站位，按照自己的意图把球发到对方球台上。

发球的方法是多种多样的，按形式来划分，可分为低抛发球（low toss serve）、高抛发球（high toss serve）和下蹲式发球（squatting serve）；按方位来划分，可分为正手发球（forehand serve）、反手发球（backhand serve）和侧身发球（sideways serve）；按性质来划分，可分为速度类发球（serving of speed）、落点类发球（serving of placement）、旋转类发球（serving of spin），如侧上旋（topspin with sidespin）、侧下旋（backspin with sidespin）、转与不转（spin or non-spin）、长球（deep serve）、短球（short serve）等。

下面选择几种主要的发球技术加以分述。

## （一）平击发球（Flat serve）

### 1. 动作特点与运用（characteristics and application）

平击发球分正手平击发球（forehand flat serve）和反手平击发球（backhand flat serve）两种，它是一种运动速度较慢、力量轻、旋转弱的一般上旋球，是初学者最基本的发球方法，也是掌握其他复杂发球方法的基础。

（1）正手平击发球（forehand flat serve）

【动作结构要领】

①选位：近台中间偏左处，左脚稍前。

Ready position：Stand in the position of the left-center of the short court and move your left leg slightly forward.

②引拍：左手将球抛起，同时拍面稍前倾，向右侧上方引拍。

Backswing：Throw up the ball with your left hand，at the same time，lean the racket slightly forward and move the racket to the upper right side of your body.

③击球：在球的下降期，向左前方发力，击球中上部。

Stroke：In the falling stage of the ball，move racket to the left front to hit the upper position of the ball.

④跟随：手臂继续向左前方随势挥动。

Follow-through：Continue to wave your arm to the left front.

⑤还原：松肩沉肘，迅速还原成击球前的准备姿势。

Recovery：Relax shoulder and lower elbow，and recover quickly to the ready position.

（2）反手平击发球（backhand flat serve）

【动作结构要领】

①选位：近台中间偏左，右脚稍前。

Ready position：Stand in the position of the left-center of the short court and move your right leg slightly forward.

②引拍：左手将球抛起，拍面前倾，向身体左侧上方引拍。

Backswing：Throw up the ball with your left hand, lean the racket slightly forward and move the racket to the upper left side of your body.

③击球：在球的下降期，向右前方发力，击球中上部。

Stroke：In the falling stage of the ball, move racket to the right front to hit the upper point of the ball.

④跟随：手臂继续向右前方随势挥动。

Follow-through：Continue to wave your arm to the right front.

⑤还原：松肩沉肘，迅速还原成击球前的准备姿势。

Recovery：Relax shoulder and lower elbow, and recover quickly to the ready position.

### 2. 易见错误( misstep)

引拍不够充分，击球时机过早。

Backswing is short, and stroke timing is too early.

### 3. 纠正( correction)

转动身体用腰带动手臂引拍，在球从高点下降至稍高于球网时击球。

Rotate upper body to bring the backswing with arm and hit the ball when it is dropping to a slightly high point above the net.

## (二)奔球( Force contact serve)

### 1. 动作特点与运用( characteristics and application)

奔球分正手奔球( forehand force contact serve)和反手奔球( backhand force contact serve)两种，它的特点是球速快、落点长、冲力强、球的飞行弧线低。在比赛中，可运用奔球的速度和落点变化干扰对手，伺机抢攻。在对付削球类打法选手时，可先迫使其退后防守，再结合摆短( drop shot)打乱其击球节奏，起到战术多变的作用。

(1)正手奔球( forehand force contact serve)

【动作结构要领】(如图3-1所示)

①选位：近台中间偏左处，左脚稍前。

Ready position：Stand in the position of left-center of the short court and move your left leg slightly forward.

②引拍：左手将球抛起，同时右臂外旋，使拍面前倾，向身体右后方引拍。

Backswing：Throw up the ball with your left hand, lean the racket slightly forward and move your fight arm to the right side behind body.

③击球：在球的下降期击球的中上部，运用手腕抖动向左前方发力。

Stroke：In the falling stage of the ball, hit the upper point of the ball to pull it to the left front, with the wrist instomtaneously move.

④跟随：手臂继续向左前方随势挥动。

Follow-through：Continue to wave your arm to the left front.

⑤还原：松肩沉肘，迅速还原成击球前的准备姿势。

Recovery：Relax shoulder and lower elbow, and recover quickly to the ready position.

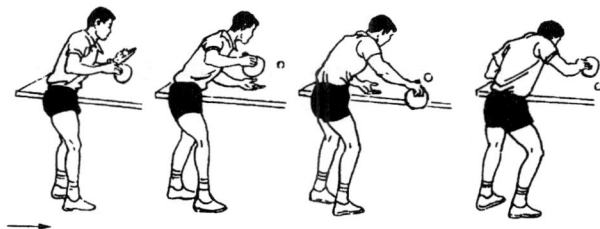

图 3-1 正手发奔球

（2）反手奔球（backhand force contact serve）

【动作结构要领】

①选位：近台中间偏左处，右脚稍前。

Ready position：Stand in the position of left center of the short court and move your left leg slightly forward.

②引拍：左手将球抛起，同时拍面前倾，向身体左后方引拍。

Backswing：Throw up the ball with your left hand, lean the racket slightly forward and move your right arm to the left side behind body.

③击球：在球的下降期击球的中上部，触球瞬间运用手腕的抖动向前方发力。

Stroke：In the falling stage of the ball, hit the upper point of the ball to pull it to the front, with the wrist instantaneously move.

④跟随：手臂继续向右前方随势挥动。

Follow-through：Continue to wave your arm to the right front.

⑤还原：松肩沉肘，迅速还原成击球前的准备姿势。

Recovery：Relax shoulder and lower elbow, and recover quickly to the ready position.

### 2. 易见错误(misstep)

握拍过紧，只运用了转腰的力量，球速不够快。

Grip is too tight, and there is only force from rotation of waist. Speed of the ball is not fast enough.

### 3. 纠正(correction)

放松身体，击球瞬间运用手腕弹击的力量。

Relax your body and hit the ball with a flick wrist.

## (三)正手发转与不转球(Forehand spin or non-spin serve)

### 1. 动作特点与运用(characteristics and application)

发球者用正手以相似的动作发出旋转强弱差异较大的球，这种球速度慢，前冲力小。在比赛中，转与不转配套使用，以旋转变化迷惑对方，破坏对方接发球战术，造成对方判断错误，可伺机抢攻或直接得分。

(1)正手发加转下旋球(forehand heavy backspin serve)

【动作结构要领】(如图 3 - 2 所示)

①选位：近台中间偏左处，左脚略在右脚前。

Ready position：Stand in the position of left-center of the short court, and move your left foot in front of right foot.

②引拍：左手将球抛起，同时握拍手腕略向外展，拍面后仰，向身体右后方引拍。

Backswing：Throw up the ball with your left hand and lean the racket slightly backward to the right side behind body.

③击球：右臂从身体右后上方向左前下方挥动，触球瞬间手腕放松摩擦球的中下部。

Stroke：Wave your right arm from the right upper side behind body to the down front. Once hitting the ball, relax wrist and brush the bottom of the ball.

④跟随：手臂继续向左前下方随势挥动。

Follow-through：Continue to wave your arm to the front downward.

⑤还原：松肩沉肘，迅速还原成击球前的准备姿势。

Recovery：Relax shoulder and lower elbow, and recover quickly to the ready position.

（2）正手发不转球（forehang non‐spin serve）

【动作结构要领】

动作结构与正手发加转下旋球大致相同，主要区别在于：击球时球拍后仰幅度略小，击球点更靠近球的中部。

图3-2　正手发加转下旋球

**2. 易见错误（misstep）**

击球点不准确，转与不转不清晰。

The hitting point is wrong. Serve with spin or non-spin is not clear.

**3. 纠正（correction）**

瞄准正确的击球部位击球。

Aim at the right position to hit the ball.

## （四）反手发转与不转球（Backhand spin or non-spin serve）

**1. 动作特点与运用（characteristics and application）**

与正手发转与不转球基本相同，一般横拍两面攻打法的选手多采用此种发球方法。在落点上运用斜线、直线与长球、短球的巧妙结合，有利于第三板抢攻。

（1）反手发加转下旋球（backhand heavy backspin serve）

【动作结构要领】

①选位：近台中间偏左处，右脚稍前，左脚稍后。

Ready position：Stand in the position of left-center of the short court, and right foot is slightly in front of left foot.

②引拍：左手将球抛起，拍面后仰，向身体左后上方引拍。

Backswing：Throw up the ball with your left hand and lean the racket backward to the upper side behind body.

③击球：右臂从身体左后上方向右前下方挥动，触球瞬间手腕放松，摩擦球的中下部。

Stroke：Wave your right arm from the left upper side behind body to the down front. Once hitting the ball, relax wrist and brush the bottom of the ball.

④跟随：手臂继续向右前下方随势挥动。

Follow-through：Continue to wave your arm to the front downward.

⑤还原：松肩沉肘，迅速还原成击球前的准备姿势。

Recovery：Relax shoulder and lower elbow, and recover quickly to the ready position.

（2）反手发不转球（backhand non – spin serve）

【动作结构要领】

动作结构与反手发加转下旋球大致一样。主要区别在于：击球时球拍后仰幅度略小，击球点更靠近球的中部。

**2. 易见错误( misstep)**

击球点错误，发不出转与不转。

The contacting point is wrong. Serve with spin or non-spin is not clear.

**3. 纠正( correction)**

引拍动作要一致。

Backswing should be coordinating.

## （五）正手发左侧下（上）旋球（Forehand left backspin/topspin with sidespin serve）

### 1. 动作特点与运用( characteristics and application)

这种发球以旋转变化为主，飞行弧线向对方左侧偏拐，对方用平挡回击也向左侧上（下）反弹。它的动作幅度较小，出手快，两种发球动作相似，有一定隐蔽性，是运动员在比赛中运用较多的发球方法。

（1）正手发左侧下旋球（forehand left backspin with sidespin serve）

【动作结构要领】（如图 3 - 3 所示）

①选位：近台中间偏左处，左脚稍前右脚在侧后。

Ready position：Stand in the position of left-center of the short court, and left foot is slightly in front of right foot.

②引拍：左手将球抛起，同时持拍手手腕略向外展，拍面后仰，转动身体向右后上方引拍。

图 3 - 3　正手发左侧下旋球

Backswing：Throw up the ball with your left hand, lean the racket back forward and rotate upper body backward.

③击球：当球从高点下降至接近网高时，转动身体，右臂从身体右后上方向左前下方挥动，击球中下部向球的左侧上方摩擦。

Stroke：When the ball falls near to the net, rotate upper body and wave right arm from the right upper side behind the body to the down front to hit the bottom of the ball and brush the left upper side of the ball.

④跟随：手臂继续向左前下方随势挥动。

Follow-through：Continue to wave your arm to the left front.

⑤还原：松肩沉肘，迅速还原成击球前的准备姿势。

Recovery：Relax shoulder and lower elbow, and recover quickly to the ready position.

（2）正手发左侧上旋球（forehand left topspin with sidespin serve）

【动作结构要领】

动作结构与正手发左侧下旋球大致一样。主要区别在于：引拍向右后上方，手臂向左前上方挥摆，击球中下部，向左侧下方向摩擦。

## 2. 易见错误（misstep）

击球时击球点选择不正确。

The hitting point is wrong.

## 3. 纠正(correction)

击球中下部并向左侧上方摩擦。

Make friction contact below center to left side. Hit the bottom of the ball and brush the left upper side of the ball.

## (六)反手发右侧上(下)旋球(Backhand right topspin/backspin with sidespin serve)

### 1. 动作特点与运用(characteristics and application)

反手发右侧上(下)旋球与正手发左侧上(下)旋球基本相同。飞行弧线向对方右侧偏拐,对方用平挡回击也向右侧上(下)反弹。

(1)反手发右侧上旋球(backhand right topspin with sidespin serve)

【动作结构要领】(如图3-4、图3-5所示)

图3-4　直拍反手发右侧上旋球

图3-5　横拍反手发右侧上旋球

①选位:近台中间偏左处,右脚稍前或两脚平行。

Ready position：Stand in the position of the left-center of the short court, and right foot is slightly in front of left foot or both feet are parallel.

②引拍:左手将球抛起同时右手手腕适当内旋,拍面后仰转动身体向左后上方引拍。

Backswing：Throw up the ball with your left hand, racket wrist is laid back slightly, rotate upper body to left and lean the racket backward and move to the left-backward backswing.

③击球：当球从高点下降至接近网高时，转动身体右臂从身体左后上方向前下方挥动。击球中下部向球的右侧上方摩擦。

Stroke：When the ball falls near to the net, rotate upper body and wave right arm from the right upper side behind the body to the down front to hit the bottom of the ball and brush the right upper side of the ball.

④跟随：手臂继续向右前下方随势挥动。

Follow-through：Continue to move your arm to the right front.

⑤还原：松肩沉肘，迅速还原成击球前的准备姿势。

Recovery：Relax shoulder and lower elbow, and recover quickly to the ready position.

（2）反手发右侧下旋球（backhand right backspin with sidespin serve）

【动作结构要领】（如图 3 - 6、图 3 - 7 所示）

图 3 - 6　直拍反手发右侧下旋球

图 3 - 7　横拍反手发右侧下旋球

动作结构与正手发左侧上旋大致相同。主要区别在于：击球时球拍从球的左侧中下部向右侧下部摩擦。

**2. 易见错误（misstep）**

击球时机过早。

Hitting time is too early.

### 3. 纠正(correction)

当球从高点下降至接近网高时击球。

Hit the ball while the ball is dropping to net height.

## (七)反手发急下旋球(Backhand fast and heavy backspin)

### 1. 动作特点与运用(characteristics and application)

球速较快并带有下旋，飞行弧线低、落点长，对方用推、拨回接容易造成下网失误，用搓球回接容易出现机会球。此种发球在比赛中只能做配合及牵制作用。

【动作结构要领】(如图3-8所示)

①选位：近台中间偏左处，左脚稍前或两脚平行。

Ready position：Stand in the position of the left-center of the short court, and left foot is slightly in front of right foot or both feet are parallel.

②引拍：抛球同时向身体左后上方引拍，拍面稍后仰。

Backswing：Throw up the ball and lean the racket slightly backward.

③击球：当球从高点下降至低于网高时，前臂迅速用力向前下方推球，摩擦球的中下部，使球第一落点接近端线。

Stroke：When the ball falls to the point lower than the net, pull the ball to the down front and brush the botton of the ball to make it near to the end line.

④跟随：手臂继续向左前下方随势挥动。

Follow-through：Continue to wave your arm to the left front.

⑤还原：松肩沉肘，迅速还原成击球前的准备姿势。

Recovery：Relax shoulder and lower elbow, and recover quickly to the ready position.

图3-8　直拍反手发急下旋球

**2. 易见错误( misstep )**

击球时机过早，第一落点太靠近网前。

Hitting time is too early, and the first bounce is close to the net.

**3. 纠正( correction )**

在球下降至低于网高时击球，第一落点靠近端线。

Hit while ball is descending to net height, and the first bounce is near to the end line.

# （八）高抛发球( High toss serve )

**1. 动作特点与运用( characteristics and application )**

发球时发球员将球向上抛 2～3 m 甚至更高，利用球下落时的速度增大对球拍的压力，从而加快了出球的速度和突然性，增大对方接发球的难度。它具有出手快、旋转强、变化多的特点。

【动作结构要领】( 如图 3 - 9 所示 )

①选位：近台中间偏左处，左脚稍前右脚在侧后。

图 3 - 9　侧身正手高抛式发球

Ready position：Stand in the position of the left-center of the short court, and left foot is slightly in front of right foot.

②引拍：左手将球抛至 2～3 m 高，同时持拍手手腕略向外展，拍面后仰，转动身体向右后上方引拍。

Backswing：Toss ball up to 2～3 m with left hand and wrist is slightly open. Rotate upper body to right side, lean racket backward and move to the right backward.

③击球：当球从高点下降至接近网高时，转动身体，右臂从身体右后上向左前下方挥动，击球中下部向球的左侧上方摩擦。

Stroke：When the ball falls near to the net, rotate upper body to right, bring right arm to the left-front direction, and brush the left upper side of the ball.

④跟随：手臂继续向左前下方随势挥动。

Follow-through：Continue to wave your arm to the left downward.

⑤还原：松肩沉肘，迅速还原成击球前的准备姿势。

Recovery：Relax shoulder and lower elbow, and recover quickly to the ready position.

高抛发球与低抛正手发左侧上（下）旋球和反手发右侧上（下）旋球基本相同，区别在于：由于球抛起高度较高，在击球时球速较快可以加快球的出手速度。

**2. 易见错误( misstep)**

抛球离身体太远，没垂直向上抛球。
Ball is not tossed vertically and far away from body.

**3. 纠正( correction)**

靠近身体垂直向上抛球。
Ball is tossed vertically and near body.

# （九）下蹲式发球( Squatting serve)

## 1. 动作特点与运用( characteristics and application)

下蹲式发球在摩擦球的部位和方向与站立式发球不同，下蹲式发球时球拍多摩擦球的上半部，发出球的旋转性能和常规发球不同，具有旋转变化多、突然性和新异性强等特点，在关键时刻可起到出其不意的效果，一般多为横拍选手采用。

（1）下蹲发右侧上旋球（squatting right topspin with sidespin serve）

【动作结构要领】（如图 3 – 10、图 3 – 11 所示）

图 3 – 10　直拍下蹲发右侧上旋球

图 3 – 11　横拍下蹲发右侧上旋球

①选位：左脚稍前或两脚平行，身体向左稍倾斜。

Ready position：Left foot is slightly forward or both feet are parallel, and body leans left slightly.

②引拍：左手将球抛起同时做下蹲姿势，右臂上举比肩高，手腕外展，拍面方向略向左偏斜。

Backswing：Throw up the ball with left hand, and body squats with right arm raised higher than shoulder. Wrist is entered and lean the racket left slightly.

③击球：当球从高点下降至接近网高时，前臂加速从左向右前方挥动。击球中部向右侧上方摩擦。

Stroke：When the ball falls near to the net, wave your forearm to the right front. Hit the center of the ball and brush the right upper side of the ball.

④跟随：手臂继续向右前上方随势挥动。

Follow-through：Continue to wave your arm to the right front.

⑤还原：松肩沉肘，迅速还原成击球前的准备姿势。

Recovery：Relax shoulder and lower elbow, and recover quickly to the ready position.

下蹲发右侧下旋球与发上旋球的动作结构大致相同。主要区别在于：击球中上部向右侧下方摩擦。

（2）下蹲发左侧上旋球（squatting left topspin with sidespin serve）

【动作结构要领】

①选位：两脚平行，身体正对球台。

Ready position：Feet are parallel, and body is towards table.

②引拍：左手将球抛起同时做下蹲姿势右臂向右下方引拍，手腕内收。

Backswing：Throw up the ball with your left hand while squatting down and move right arm to the right downward. Wrist is laid back.

③击球：当球从高点下降至接近网高时，前臂加速从右下方向左前上方挥动。击球中部向左侧上方摩擦。

Stroke：When the ball falls near to the net, move forearm to the left front with acceleration. Hit the center of the ball and brush the left upper side of the ball.

④跟随：手臂继续向左前上方随势挥动。

Follow-through：Continue to wave your arm to the left front.

⑤还原：松肩沉肘，迅速还原成击球前的准备姿势。

Recovery：Relax shoulder and lower elbow, and recover quickly to the ready position.

下蹲发左侧下旋球与发上旋球的动作结构大致相同。主要区别在于：击球中上部向左侧下方摩擦。

## 2. 易见错误（misstep）

击球时机过早，使发球弧线过高。

Timing is too early. The path of serve is too high.

## 3. 纠正（correction）

降低重心在球下降至接近网高时击球。

Lower weight and hit while the ball is descending to net height.

## （十）逆旋转发球（Reverse spin serve）

### 1. 动作特点与运用（characteristics and application）

逆旋转发球是近年来在原先顺旋转发球的基础上发明的一项新发球技术。其动作隐蔽，出手迅速，发力协调，旋转较强而富有变化，用正手发出的球能具有类似反手发球的性质，特别适合于反手强的选手发球后两面上手抢攻。

【动作结构要领】

①选位：近台中间偏左处，左脚稍前右脚在侧后。

Ready position：Stand in the position of left side of the short court, and left foot is slight in front of right foot.

②引拍：引拍后肘部抬起，手腕向内后引动。

Backswing：Raise elbow and turn wrist to body with the racket pointing to breast.

③击球：当球从高点下降至接近网高时，摩擦球的外侧部。发侧下旋球时，击球的中下部，发侧上旋球时，触球的左侧上部。

Stroke：When the ball falls near to the net, brush the outside of the ball. If it is backspin with sidespin serve, hit the ball downward. If it is topspin with sidespin serve, hit the left upper side of the ball.

④跟随：手臂继续随势挥动。

Follow-through：Continue to wave your arm.

⑤还原：松肩沉肘，迅速还原成击球前的准备姿势。

Recovery：Relax shoulder and lower elbow, and recover quickly to the ready position.

### 2. 易见错误（misstep）

手肘抬起不够，球发出去旋转不强。

The elbow is not raised enough, and the spin is not heavy.

### 3. 纠正（correction）

手肘向后抬起，前臂配合手腕协调发力。

The elbow is raised backward, and the forearm and wrist snap in coordinating way.

# 三、接发球(Return of service)

在比赛中,相对其他环节而言,接发球的难度最大,因为接发球方对发球方在技术上没有任何限制的方法,这样一来就大大增加了接发球的预测难度。比赛中如接发球不好,自己的技战术也无法发挥。所以不断提高接发球的能力,合理地把掌握的技术运用到接发球中,是迅速提高比赛实战能力的关键。

## (一)接发球的站位(The stance of the receiving)

首先,必须根据对方发球的站位(server position)来决定自己的站位。其次,站位还要考虑是否能为本方直接进攻创造一定的有利条件。一般来讲,如果对方站在球台左半台(left half court),本方也应该在球台的左半台;若对方站在球台的右半台(right half court),本方也应相应调整至球台的中间偏右位置。总之接发球的站位选择,既要考虑对方来球落点(placement)的变化,还要保证自己个人技术特长的发挥。

## (二)对来球性能的判断(Judging the type of the coming ball)

### 1. 对来球旋转的判断(judging the spin of the coming ball)

乒乓球发球中常出现的旋转主要有左侧上、下旋,右侧上、下旋,转与不转等,并通过发球者利用各种发球方式,将这些旋转性质表现出来。如用正、反手发球、高抛发球和下蹲发球等。在判断旋转性质时,可以从以下几个方面进行考虑。

(1)拍形(racket angel):发上旋球时,拍形比较竖,发下旋球时比较平、斜。这种特点与发球时要接触球的部位直接发生关系,因为发旋转球和不转球时,接触点比较靠近球的中后部;而发侧下旋和下旋时,向中下部和底部摩擦球才可能比较转。

(2)动作轨迹(the movement of forehand and wrist):发上旋和不转球时,球与球拍接触的一瞬间,手腕摆动的幅度一般不是很大,并时常与假动作配合。在发侧下旋和下旋球时,手腕摆动相对大一点,这样容易"吃"住球,动作也比较固定,击球后常有一个停顿,即使加上假动作,也不会像发侧上旋球和不转球那样连贯。

(3)来球弧线(path of coming ball):上旋球和不转球的运行一般较快,常有往前"窜拱"的感觉,发短球时容易出台,弧线低平;下旋球运行比较平稳,弧线略高,短球不易出台。

(4)出手速度(the contacting speed):发上旋球和不转球一般出手比较快,并且动作突然;下旋球的出手相对慢一些,因为要给球以足够的摩擦时间,才能使球产生强烈的下旋效果。

**2. 对速度和落点的判断(judging speed and placement on the serve)**

(1)长球(deep serve)的第一落点多在本方台面的端线(end line)附近。如果力量差不多,侧上旋和不转球的运行速度明显要快于侧下旋和下旋球;如果是发侧上旋(topspin with sidespin)、侧下旋(backspin with sidespin)斜线长球,要注意球的第二弧线有侧拐的特点。如果是直线长球,要注意平推过来,或者是略带外拐的球,因为这种球除了有很快的速度外,容易发出线路比较直的球,客观上增加了球的角度,给接发球者造成较大的难度。

(2)发球方想要把球发短,手上就不能发很大的力,要收住一点,所以短球比较难发挥速度的优势,比较多的是考虑球的落点和旋转,可根据这一特点判断来球的长短。在接短球时,要特别注意手臂不要过早地深入台内,以免侧上旋短球的第二弧线往前"拱",顶在板上,使手上失去对球的控制,以及来球可能是"小三角"位置,球是从近网的边线(side line)出台,手来不及拿下来,对不准球。

(3)对半出台球(mid-depth serve)的判断是接发球(return of service)判断中难度比较大的一项技术。因为这种球往往容易造成接发球者的犹豫,使思路混乱,影响整场比赛的发挥。在判断这种球时,一是视其旋转性质而定,侧上旋和不转球比侧下旋和下旋球容易出台;二是根据发球者的特点而定,要仔细研究发球者在发半出台球时,到底哪种容易出台,哪种不容易出台,是正手容易出台还是反手容易出台等。这样就会增加接半出台球选择方法的针对性。

## (三)接发球的方法(Methods of receiving)

接发球的方法很多,它是由点(flip)、拨(backhand stroke)、推(block)、拉(loop)、搓(push)、削(chop)、摆短(drop shot)、撇侧旋(push aside)、挑(hit forward and up)等多种综合性技术组成的。只有比较全面地掌握各种接发球的方法,才能在比赛中减少被动,多些主动。下面针对来球的不同性质介绍常用的接发球技术。

**1. 接急球(returning fast-moving serve)**

对于反手位的急球,不宜采用侧身的办法回接,一般用反手推(backhand

block）和反手攻（backhand attack）来回接。正手位的急球用正手快带、快攻借力回接。如果采用削球回接，要注意先向后移动，等来球速度和力量减弱时再削。如对方发过来的是急下旋球（heavy backspin），用推或攻回接时，应调节好拍形，使拍面稍后仰，增加向上的发力。用弧圈球回接，也应增加向上提拉（lift）的力量。用搓球（push）回接，首先要向后退位，注意拍面角度不要后仰过大，击住球的中部向下发力，以抵消来球的前进力。

**2. 接下旋球（returning backspin serve）**

用搓球回接时，注意拍面后仰，增加向前上方的发力。用拉攻或弧圈回接时一定要增加向上提拉的力量。用突击回击时，要充分借力，注意击球时机的把握，拍形要调节好前倾的角度，手腕要掌握好向前向上向内的尺度。采用拨、拧都要注意拍形的调整和向上的力度把握。

**3. 接左侧上（下）旋球（returning left topspin/backspin with sidespin serve）**

接左侧上旋球，一般适宜用推、攻回击比较。回接时，拍面角度要适当前倾，拍面所朝方向要向左偏斜（left skew），用来抵消来球的左侧旋转，向前下方用力要相对加大，防止球触拍时向自己的右上方反弹。如用搓削回接，除注意拍面角度和所朝方向外，还要加大向下摩擦球的力量。用弧圈回接时，要加大球拍前倾的角度，要多向前发力，少向上提拉。

接左侧下旋球，一般适宜采用搓、削回击。回接时，拍面角度要适当后仰，拍面所朝方向要向左偏斜。击球时要稍向上用力，防止球拍触球时向自己的左下方反弹。如用推、攻来接，除注意拍面角度和所朝方向外，还要加大向上摩擦球的力量。用弧圈回接时，要注意拍面角度不易过度前倾，要多向上提拉，少向前发力。

**4. 接右侧上（下）旋球（returning right topspin/backspin with sidespin）**

接右侧上旋球，一般采用推、攻为宜。回接时，拍面角度要稍前倾，拍面所朝方向向右偏斜以抵消（counteract）来球的右侧旋转，向前下方用力要相对加大，防止球触拍时向自己左上方反弹（rebound）。如用搓、削回接，除注意拍面角度和所朝方向外，还要加大向下摩擦的力量。用弧圈球（loop）回接要加大拍面前倾角度，多向前发力，少向下提拉。

右侧下旋球是右侧旋与下旋结合的旋转球，接这种球一般采用搓、削回击为宜。回接时，拍面角度要稍向后仰，拍面所朝方向向右偏斜以抵消来球的右侧旋，向上用力要相对大，防止球触拍时向自己左下方反弹。如用推、攻回接，除注意拍面角度和所朝方向外，还要加大向上摩擦(friction)球的力量。用弧圈球回接时要注意拍面角度不宜过度前倾，多向上用力提拉，少向前发力。

**5. 接短球(returning short serve)**

由于对方发过来的球是台内近网短球，回接时，最主要的是注意及时上前，以获得最合适的击球位置。同时要控制好身体的前冲力量，接发球后要迅速还原(recover)，准备后续击球。无论用搓、削、攻、拉哪种方法回接短球，都应该特别注意来球是在台内，受台面空间的制约，不可能充分引拍，因此要注重充分发挥前臂(forearm)和手腕(wrist)的动作，同时要根据来球的旋转性能，调节拍面的角度，找准击球部位，把握击球时机和用力的方向。

# 四、推挡球技术(The techniques of block)

推挡球技术在直板快攻选手中是一门非常重要的技术，有时在比赛中使用反手的机会多于正手，尤其在相持摆速时更是经常使用的重要技术。它的特点是离台近、球速快、动作小、变化多。在相持对攻中可以使用快推或加力推结合落点变化来调动对方位置，争取主动；有时也可以用它来牵制对方，为正手进攻或侧身进攻，创造较有利的时机。在掌握和运用推挡技术时，必须要求做到速度快、变化多、力量大。常用的推挡球技术有平挡球、快推球、加力推、减力挡、推下旋球、推侧旋球、反手快拨等。

## (一)平挡球(Flat block)

### 1. 动作特点与运用(characteristics and application)

球速慢、力量轻、动作较简单，初学者容易掌握。它可以帮助初学者熟悉球性，认识乒乓球的击球规律，提高控制球的能力。

【动作结构要领】

①选位：身体离台30~50 cm，两脚开立与肩同宽。

Ready position：Keep away from the table about 30~50 cm and stand with your feet shoulder-width apart.

②引拍：上臂应靠近身体，前臂与台面平行，球拍呈半横状，拍面垂直球台，将球拍引至身体的前方。

Backswing：Keep upper arm close to body, forearm parallel to the table, racket pointing to side and standing vertically above the table, bring racket to the front of the body.

③击球：借助来球的反弹力，在来球的上升期击球的中部。

Stroke：Hit center of the ball when it is rising.

④跟随：手臂和手腕随势前送。

Follow-through：Continue to move arm and wrist.

⑤还原：松肩沉肘，迅速还原成击球前的准备姿势。

Recovery：Relax shoulder and lower elbow, and recover quickly to the ready position.

### 2. 易犯错误(misstep)

判断落点不准、拍面掌握不好。

The judgement of placement and angle of racket in block are easy to be wrong.

### 3. 纠正(correction)

提高判断能力，加强手腕的灵活性和提高调整拍面的能力。

Improve the ability of judgement, and strengthen the flexibility of wrist and the ability to adjust racket angle.

## (二)快推球(Fast block)

### 1. 动作特点与运用(characteristic and application)

快推球具有站位近、动作小、球速快、变化多等特点，既可积极防守，又可辅助进攻。适用于回击一般的拉球、推挡球和攻球。

【动作结构要领】(如图 3 – 12 所示)

①选位：身体离台约 40 cm，站立于左半台，左脚稍前。

Ready position：Keep away from the table about 40 cm, and stand at the left side of the table with left foot forward.

②引拍：击球前肘关节靠近身体，上臂适当地往后引拍，前臂稍作外旋面前倾。

Backswing：Keep elbow joint close to body, the upper arm back and forearm open with racket leaning backward.

③击球：来球时，手腕压拍，手臂迅速向前迎球，在来球的高点期击球中上部。

Stroke：Use wrist to press the racket, move arm to hit the ball and hit the upper side of the ball when it is rising to peak.

④跟随：触球后，肘关节继续前迎，手腕随势送出。

Follow-through：Continue to move elbow joint and wrist after contacting.

⑤还原：松肩沉肘，迅速还原成击球前的准备姿势。

Recovery：Relax shoulder and lower elbow, and recover quickly to the ready position.

**2. 易犯错误（misstep）**

击球过程中重心不稳。

The weight is unbalanced when hitting the ball.

**3. 纠正（correction）**

动作过程中，身体重心放在双脚上。

Put weight on feet when moving.

图 3 - 12　快推球

## （三）加力推（Punch block）

**1. 动作特点与运用（characteristics and application）**

加力推具有回球力量重、速度快等特点。比赛时可以加力推对手的远台，迫使对方离台，让对方陷入被动防守的局面。

【动作结构要领】（如图 3 - 13 所示）

①选位：身体离台约 40 cm，站立于左半台，左脚稍前。

Ready position：Keep away from the table about 40 cm, and stand at the left side of the table with left foot forward.

②引拍：上臂随着腰和髋的右转往后引拍，前臂稍作外旋，食指用力压球拍，使拍面保持前倾。

Backswing：Rotate waist and hip to right and move upper arm to the right behind body. The forearm is laid back with forefinger fasten racket in closed way.

③击球：肘关节在髋和腰的转动下，加速往前送出，同时手腕发力，在球的上升后期击球的中上部。

Stroke：Followed by rotation of hip and waist, the elbow joint is pushed forward with acceleration. Hit the upper side of the ball when it is rising to peak.

④跟随：手臂和手腕继续向前下方随势送出。

Follow-through：Continue to move forearm and wrist.

⑤还原：松肩沉肘，迅速还原成击球前的准备姿势。

Recovery：Relax shoulder and lower elbow, and recover quickly to the ready position.

### 2. 易犯错误(misstep)

手臂没有向前伸出。
The arm is not pushed forward.

### 3. 纠正(correction)

强调击球后上臂和肘关节前送。
Make sure that upper arm and elbow joint are pushed forward.

图 3 - 13　直拍反手加力推球

## (四)减力挡(Cushion block)

### 1. 动作特点与运用(characteristics and application)

回击球时，具有落点短、力量轻、球速慢等特点。是直拍选手对付弧圈球的一种很好的方法，减力挡可以将来球的力量卸掉一部分，从而减少回球的力量，减短回球的飞行轨迹，使对方无法连续拉弧圈球或是打乱对方拉弧圈球的节奏，造成回球主动失误。

【动作结构要领】（如图 3 – 14 所示）

①选位：身体离台约 40 cm，站立于左半台，左脚稍前。

Ready position：Keep away from the table about 40 cm, and stand at the left side of the table with left foot forward.

②引拍：上臂靠近身体，前臂与台面几乎平行，拍面前倾，引拍至小腹前。

Backswing：Keep upper arm close to body, forearm almost parallel with the table and lean the racket forward and move to front of abdomen.

③击球：击球瞬间手臂和手腕向后收，卸掉一部分来球的力量，在来球的上升期触球的中上部。

Stroke：Forearm and wrist are laid back to reduce force from the opponent's stroke, and hitting the upper side of the ball when it is rising.

④跟随：手臂和手腕继续向后随势收回。

Follow-through：Continue to move arm and wrist backward.

⑤还原：松肩沉肘，迅速还原成击球前的准备姿势。

Recovery：Relax shoulder and lower elbow, and recover quickly to the ready position.

图 3 – 14　直拍反手减力挡球

## 2. 易犯错误（misstep）

减力时，前臂和手腕不协调。

Arm and wrist are incoordinated to reduce force from the opponent's stroke.

## 3. 纠正（correction）

球拍击球瞬间，前臂和手腕轻轻后移，以减小来球的反弹力。

Move arm and wrist backward slightly while hitting the ball to reduce force from the opponent's stroke.

## （五）推下旋球（Backspin block）

### 1. 动作特点与运用（characteristics and application）

推下旋球适用于对付上旋不强、力量不大的来球。其回球速度较快且呈下旋，容易使对方判断失误，从而直接得分或创造更好的进攻机会。

【动作结构要领】（如图 3－15 所示）

图 3－15　直拍反手推下旋球

①选位：身体离台约 40 cm，站立于左半台，左脚稍前。

Ready position：Keep away from the table about 40 cm, and stand at the left side of the table with left foot forward.

②引拍：肘关节下沉，前臂上举，引拍略高，拍面稍后仰。

Backswing：Lower elbow joint while raising forearm. Backswing is slightly high with the racket leaning backward.

③击球：在上臂和前臂的带动发力下，手腕向下做推切动作，在来球高点期或下降前期摩擦球的中下部。

Stroke：Hitting the bottom of the ball when it is rising to peak or beginning to descend, with the upper arm and forearm coordinatelya, wrist move and chop down.

④跟随：手臂和手腕继续往前下方推出。

Follow-through：Arm and wrist continue to be pushed to the front downward direction.

⑤还原：松肩沉肘，迅速还原成击球前的准备姿势。

Recovery：Relax shoulder and lower elbow, and recover quickly to the ready position.

**2. 易见错误(misstep)**

摩擦球控制不到位。

Friction contact is not good.

**3. 纠正(correction)**

上臂、前臂和手腕用力使球拍向前下方摩擦球。

Use upper arm, forearm and wrist snap to make friction contact to the front downward direction.

## (六)推侧旋球(Sidespin block)

### 1. 动作特点与运用(characteristics and application)

推侧旋球也称推挤，是直拍选手对付弧圈球(loop)的一种比较稳健和有效的技术。它具有弧线低(low trajectory)、角度大等特点，并且球落台后会出现拐点。

【动作结构要领】

①选位：站位在球台中间或偏左，身体离台约40 cm，左脚稍前。

Ready position：Keep away from the table about 40 cm, and stand at the left-center of the table with left foot forward.

②引拍：右上臂和肘关节靠近身体右侧，手臂自然弯曲，前臂上提并外旋引拍至身前，使拍面稍前倾。

Backswing：Keep right upper arm and elbow joint close to the right side of body, bent arm naturally, lift and open forearm, lean racket forward and move to the front of body.

③击球：前臂和手腕向左前下方挥拍迎球，在来球的上升前期拍面前倾推击球的中上部；球拍击球瞬间，前臂和手腕向左前下方发力。

Stroke：Move forearm and wrist to the left front direction to return and lean racket forward, during it is rising to peak with forearm and wrist forward – left down.

④跟随：击球后，手腕和手臂顺势向左前下方挥动。

Follow-through：Continue to move arm and wrist to the front downward direction.

⑤还原：松肩沉肘，迅速还原成击球前的准备姿势。

Recovery：Relax shoulder and lower elbow, and recover quickly to the ready position.

### 2. 易见错误(misstep)

发力方向控制不好。

Force direction is out of control.

### 3. 纠正(correction)

球拍击球瞬间,前臂和手腕向左前下方发力。

Move forearm and wrist to the left and front direction while hitting the ball.

## (七)反手快拨(Backhand quick block)

### 1. 动作特点与运用(characteristics and application)

反手快拨主要运动特点是动作小,球速快,线路活。横拍选手多用于相持球中回击一般上旋球。

【动作结构要领】

①选位:站位近台,两脚平站或左脚略前,两膝微屈,收腹含胸,身体向前。

Ready position: Be close to the table, keep feet parallel or left foot slightly in front, bend knees and shift weight to front part of feet.

②引拍:右肩稍低,肘关节前顶,手腕内收,将球拍引至腹前偏左的位置。

Backswing: Lower right shoulder, push elbow joint forward, keep wrist closed forward and put racket toward left side of abdomen.

③击球:在来球的上升期,前臂手腕配合发力击球的中上部。

Stroke: Hit the ball when it is rising coordinated by forearm and wrist.

④跟随:击球后,前臂手腕顺势向右前上方挥出。

Follow-through: Continue to move arm and wrist to the right forward direction.

⑤还原:松肩沉肘,迅速还原成击球前的准备姿势。

Recovery: Relax shoulder and lower elbow, and recover quickly to the ready position.

### 2. 易见错误(misstep)

没有固定住手腕,手腕来回甩。

Wrist is not fixed and swings.

**3. 纠正( correction )**

多做徒手动作，先固定住手腕，在击球的瞬间，大拇指压拍，向前送球。

Do more exercise. Fix wrist firstly, then use thumb to pull the ball.

# 五、攻球技术( The technique of attack )

攻球技术是乒乓球技术中最重要的基本技术，是比赛中争取主动得分的重要手段，它具有速度快、力量大、应用范围广泛等特点。20 世纪 70 年代以来，由于国际交往和学习研究的加强，各种打法互取长短，使乒乓球技术得到了更快的发展和提高。比如，我国近台快攻、直拍快攻结合弧圈球、横拍快攻结合弧圈球等打法和技术均有所发展和创新，在国际比赛中取得了优良的成绩。不论是使用横拍还是直拍的快攻型打法的运动员，必须具备更加全面的攻球技术，才能跟得上乒乓球技术发展的形势。

攻球可分为正手攻球、反手攻球和侧身攻球。其中正手攻球主要分为快攻、快点、快带、突击、扣杀、中远台攻球、放高球、杀高球、滑板球等。反手攻球主要分为快攻、快点、快带、扣杀、中远台攻球等。我们要能够根据来球的性质，采取相应的攻球方式。作为一名乒乓球选手，只有掌握较为全面的攻球技术，这样才能更好地在场上抓住得分机会。

## ( 一 ) 正手快攻( Forehand quick attack )

### 1. 动作特点与运用( characteristics and application )

站位近、动作小、出手快，借球的反弹力还击球，与落点变化相结合，可调动对方为扣杀创造条件。是近台快攻打法的一项主要技术。

【动作结构要领】( 如图 3 - 16、图 3 - 17 所示 )

①选位：身体离台大概 40 cm，两脚开立与肩同宽或稍宽，左脚稍前，两膝微屈，重心压向前脚掌。

Ready position：Keep away from the table about 40 cm, stand with feet shoulder-width apart or wider, bend knees and shift weight to front part of feet and place right foot slightly behind left foot.

②引拍：在腰和髋的带动下引拍至身体右侧方，大臂与身体的夹角大概在35° ~40°之间。前臂几乎与地面平行，拍面稍微前倾。

Backswing：Rotate waist and hip to bring the racket to the right side of body. The angle between upper arm and body is 35° ~ 40°, forearm is almost parallel to ground and the racket is closed forward down slightly.

③击球：在来球的上升后期击球的中上部，击球以撞击为主，然后前臂快速收缩。

Stroke：Hit the upper point of the ball when it is rising.

④跟随：顺着惯性向左上方挥拍，同时身体重心由右脚移至左脚。

Follow-through：Continue to move the racket to the left upward direction while weight is shifted from right foot to left foot.

⑤还原：松肩沉肘，迅速还原成击球前的准备姿势。

Recovery：Relax shoulder and lower elbow, and recover quickly to the ready position.

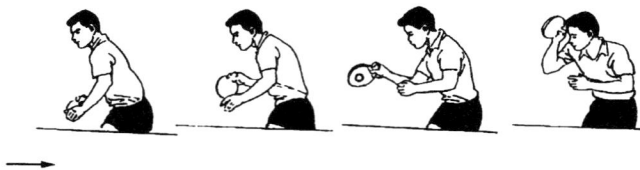

图 3 – 16　直拍正手快攻

图 3 – 17　横拍正手快攻

## 2. 易见错误( misstep)

抬肘抬臂。
Elbow and arm are raised.

### 3. 纠正（correction）

多做近台快攻练习，强调击球时肘肩沉向后下方。

Do more exercise of quick attack in short court. Lower elbow and shoulder to the backward and downward while hitting the ball.

## （二）反手快攻（Backhand quick attack）

### 1. 动作特点与运用（characteristics and application）

反手快攻技术根据握拍的方式可分为横拍反手快攻技术以及直拍的反面快拨技术。横拍反手快攻技术具有站位近、动作小、速度快、变化多等特点。它主要用来对付弧圈球、推挡球或反手攻球，是两面攻选手常用的一种主要基本技术。

直拍反面快拨技术使得直拍选手反手可以像横拍一样进攻，将反手位的球处理得更加快速、灵活。

（1）横拍反手快攻（backhand quick drive by shake-hand grip）

【动作结构要领】

①选位：右脚稍前，双脚开立与肩稍宽，身体正对来球。

Ready position：Stand with feet shoulder-width apart or wider, place left foot slightly behind right foot, and stand straightly forward to the returning.

②引拍：将身体重心移至右腿，右肩保持下沉，大臂保持稳定，腹部内收，前臂以肘部为轴向左腹引拍。

Backswing：Move weight to right leg, lower right shoulder while keeping upper arm steadily, and make forearm pivot around elbow with racket pointing to left side of abdomen.

③击球：当来球落台刚刚跳起时，腹部和前臂同时向外展开，手腕内收，在来球的上升后期或高点期击球的中部或中上部。

Stroke：Open abdomen and forearm before hitting the ball, lay wrist back and contact center or upper point of the ball when it is rising to peak.

④跟随：重心由左脚转移至右脚，手臂跟随着身体顺势挥出。

Follow-through：Shift weight from left foot to right foot and continue to move arm with body rotation.

⑤还原：松肩沉肘，迅速还原或击球前的准备姿势。

Recovery：Relax shoulder and lower elbow, and recover quickly to the ready position.

（2）直拍反面快拨（backhand quick drive by pen-hold grip）

【动作结构要领】

①选位：左脚在前，右脚稍后，两脚与肩稍宽，身体靠近球台。

Ready position：Stand with feet shoulder-width or wider，place right foot slightly behind left foot and keep body close to the table.

②引拍：两膝微屈，含胸收腹，前臂内收至胸前，与地面平行。手腕内屈，拍面前倾引至左腹前。

Backswing：Bend knees and pull stomach in，lay forearm back to breast and parallel to the ground，lay wrist back，incline the racket forward and move to the left front of abdomen.

③击球：在来球的上升期或高点期，以肘关节为中心，带动前臂与手腕，向右前方挥出。

Stroke：Make forearm and wrist pivot around elbow and move to the right front direction when the ball is rising.

④跟随：击球后，手臂随势往前送出，身体重心从右脚移至左脚。

Follow-through：Continue to move arm and shift weight from right foot to left foot.

⑤还原：松肩沉肘，迅速还原成击球前的准备姿势。

Recovery：Relax shoulder and lower elbow，and recover quickly to the ready position.

## 2. 易见错误（misstep）

（1）只注意上肢发力击球，忽视腰、髋、腿转动的力量。

There is no force from rotation of waist，hip and leg but upper limb.

（2）拍面的方向偏右，球从右边线飞出。

Ball flies out of table from right sideline with the racket pointing to right.

## 3. 纠正（correction）

（1）击球时加强腰、髋、腿的辅助力量运用。

Strengthen force from rotation of waist，hip and leg while hitting the ball.

（2）击球时将手腕后屈内旋。

Wrist is laid back while hitting the ball.

# （三）正手快点（Forehand flip）

## 1. 动作特点与运用（characteristics and application）

正手快点站位靠近球台，动作小、出手快、线路灵活，回球带有突击性。用于进攻台内球，打破对方的小球控制，可在前三板中争取更多的主动。

【动作结构要领】（如图3－18、图3－19所示）

①选位：站位时身体靠近球台，身体前倾，重心压至前脚掌。

Ready position：Be close to the table and body leans forward to rest weight on front part of feet.

②引拍：当右方大角度来球时上右脚，身体前迎，手臂自然弯曲迎前，前臂伸向台内。

Backswing：If your opponent returns from right corner, step in with right foot and bend arm naturally while forearm reaching to table inside.

③击球：根据来球旋转程度手臂相应地作内旋或外旋调整拍面角度，在来球的下降前期或高点期完成击球。

Stroke：According to the type and amount of spin, forearm is open or laid back to adjust racket angle. Hitting the ball when ball is beginning to descend.

④跟随：在台内完成击球后，重心顺势前迎，手臂挥至身前。

Follow-through：Finish stroke in table, continue weight to move and move arm back to front of body.

⑤还原：松肩沉肘，迅速还原成击球前的准备姿势。

Recovery：Relax shoulder and lower elbow, and recover quickly to the ready position.

引拍击球时，若来球下旋强（heavy backspin）时，拍面稍后仰，在下降前期击球中下部，前臂、手腕向前上方发力；下旋弱（light backspin）时，拍面垂直，击球中部，前臂、手腕发力向前为主，适当向上发力；来球上旋时，拍面稍前倾，击球中上部（above center）。

## 2. 易见错误（misstep）

手臂伸得过直，使得手腕紧张。

Extend arm too straight to strain wrist.

### 3. 纠正(correction)

身体迎球要充分，手臂自然弯曲前迎。

Make sure your body get close to the table and arm bent naturally to push forward.

图 3 – 18　直拍正手快点

图 3 – 19　横拍正手快点

## (四)反手快点(Backhand flip)

### 1. 动作特点与运用(characteristics and application)

反手快点的特点与正手快点的相似，是用于处理反手台内球的一种进攻技术，多用于前三板。如发短球后和接近网短球以及相互摆短时，常用它来抢先上手，以争取下一板的进攻机会。

【动作结构要领】

①选位：站位靠近球台，身体前倾，重心落在两脚之间。

Ready position：Be close to the table and lean forward to rest weight on middle of feet.

②引拍：左方近网来球，以左脚向左前方上步；中间偏左来球，则以右脚向前上步，身体重心前迎，同时前臂伸向台内准备击球。

Backswing：If the placement is on the left side near net, step in with left foot; If it is on the left-center of the table, move forward right foot with weight shift. Reach forearm to the table and stroke.

③击球：根据来球旋转程度适当调整手腕的内旋程度和拍面角度，如快点下旋球时，根据其下旋程度将拍形垂直或后仰，在来球的下降前期击球的中部或中下部。来球上旋时，拍面稍前倾，击球的中上部。

Stroke：According to the type and amount of spin, the receiver adjusts racket angle and the way to lay wrist back. If it is backspin, hold the racket vertically backward and hit the center or bottom of the ball when it is descending. If it is topspin, lean the racket forward slightly and hit the upper side of the ball.

④跟随：完成击球后，重心跟随前迎，手臂顺势向右上方挥出。

Follow-through：Continue to move weight and arm after hitting the ball.

⑤还原：松肩沉肘，迅速还原成击球前的准备姿势。

Recovery：Relax shoulder and lower elbow, and recover quickly to the ready position.

直拍选手在使用横打技术快点时，引拍时手腕自然下垂，大拇指(thumb)用力握住球拍，食指(forefinger)自然放松。

**2. 易见错误(misstep)**

来球的旋转判断不准确，造成出手的迟疑。

Wrong judgement of spin causes hesitation.

**3. 纠正(correction)**

击球前首先判断来球旋转的种类，其次是判断旋转的强度。

Judge the speed and amount of spin before hitting the ball.

## (五)正手快带(Forehand slightly force brush contact against drive)

**1. 动作特点与运用(characteristics and application)**

正手快带与正手攻球相似，主要利用来球的前进力量将球带出。多用来对付弧圈球，以速度快、弧线低、落点变化多，来为下一板主动进攻创造条件。

【动作结构要领】(如图 3 – 20、图 3 – 21 所示)

①选位：左脚稍前，站位较近，身体离台约 40 cm。

Ready position：Keep away from the table about 40 cm, place right foot slightly behind left foot.

②引拍：手臂自然弯曲至身体的右前方，引拍的幅度极小，拍面前倾且高于来球，手腕保持稳定。

Backswing：Bend arm to the left front side of body with a short backswing. Lean the racket forward and higher than the return and keep wrist in a steady position.

③击球：在腰和上臂的带动下，于来球的上升期击球中上部，前臂快速向左前方挥动。

Stroke：Rotate waist and upper arm. Move forearm to the left front direction and hit the upper side of the ball while the ball is rising.

④跟随：手臂继续向前上方随势挥动。

Follow-through：Continue to move arm to the front upward direction.

⑤还原：松肩沉肘，迅速还原成击球前的准备姿势。

Recovery：Relax shoulder and lower elbow, and recover quickly to the ready position.

## 2. 易见错误(misstep)

触球点离身体过远。

Hitting point is far away from body.

## 3. 纠正(correction)

引拍动作小，在球靠近身体时将球带过去。

Hit the ball when it is coming near your body with a short backswing.

图 3 - 20　横拍正手快带

图 3 - 21　直拍正手快带

## (六)反手快带(Backhand slightly force brush contact against drive)

### 1. 动作特点与运用(characteristics and application)

反手快带的特点与正手快带相同,利用来球的力量将球带出,使球速度快,弧线低,落点变化多。

【动作结构要领】

①选位:站位近台,两脚几乎成平行开立。

Ready position:Stand close to the table with feet apart and almost parallel.

②引拍:身体自然放松,前臂外旋使拍面前倾,小幅度地将球拍引至身体的左前方。

Backswing:Relax body,open forearm with the racket leaning forward and move the racket to the left front side with short backswing.

③击球:在来球的上升期,前臂借助腰和髋的转动向前迎球,击球的中上部。

Stroke:Followed by rotation of waist and hip,move forearm forward to against ball and hit the upper side of the ball when it is rising.

④跟随：击球后手臂继续顺势往前送。

Follow-through：Continue to move arm forward.

⑤还原：松肩沉肘，迅速还原成击球前的准备姿势。

Recovery：Relax shoulder and lower elbow, and recover quickly to the ready position.

### 2. 易见错误(misstep)

击球时机不准。

Timing is wrong.

### 3. 纠正(correction)

在来球的上升期击球。

Hit the ball when the ball is rising.

## (七)正手突击(Forehand sudden attack)

### 1. 动作特点与运用(characteristics and application)

正手突击具有动作小、出手快、隐蔽性强等特点，是接台内及半出台下旋球(backspin)的重要方法，也是正胶(short-pimps rubber)快攻型选手的主要得分技术。

【动作结构要领】(如图3-22所示)

①选位：两脚开立，左脚稍前，重心稍低。

Ready position：Stand with feet shoulder-width apart or wider, lower weight slightly and place right foot slightly behind left foot.

②引拍：右肩稍低，前臂自然弯曲，手腕放松，引拍至身体侧面，拍形根据下旋的强弱调整。当来球下旋强时拍面稍后仰，下旋弱时拍面垂直或稍前倾。

Backswing：Lower right shoulder and bend forearm naturally, relax wrist to bring the racket to the side of body. If the opponent returns heavy backspin, lean the racket backward slightly; if it is light backspin, hold the racket vertical or forward slightly.

③击球：手臂在腰的带动下加速收缩，在来球的高点期手腕转动摩擦球的中下部。

Stroke：Pull back forearm followed by rotation of waist and brush the bottom of the ball when it is rising.

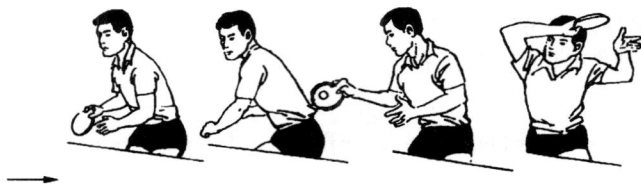

图 3 – 22　直拍正手突击

④跟随：击完球后，身体继续转过来保持重心的稳定，手臂内旋收回。

Follow-through：Continue to rotate body, keep weight in steady position after hitting the ball, and pull arm back and recover.

⑤还原：松肩沉肘，迅速还原成击球前的准备姿势。

Recovery：Relax shoulder and lower elbow, and recover quickly to the ready position.

**2. 易见错误( misstep)**

强烈下旋时习惯性使用突击。

Have a habit of sudden drive against heavy backspin.

**3. 纠正( correction)**

击球前，判断好下旋的强弱，下旋强烈时不宜采用突击。

Make judgment about intensity of spin before hitting the ball.

## (八)正手扣杀( Forehand smash)

**1. 动作特点与运用( characteristics and application)**

正手扣杀的特点是力量重，球速快，威力大。扣杀大多是在其他技术取得主动和优势或者回击对方高球的情况下才运用，并将落点变化与之相结合，往往能直接得分。

【动作结构要领】( 如图 3 – 23 所示)

①选位：根据球的落点站好位置，左脚稍前。

Ready position：According to the placement of ball, choose a good ready position with left foot slightly in front.

②引拍：手臂在腰和髋的转动下向身体的右后方引拍，拍面保持前倾。

Backswing：Followed by rotation of waist and hip, move arm to the right backward and lean the racket forward.

③击球：腰和髋向左转动配合手臂和前臂的发力，在来球的高点期击球的中上部。

Stroke：Rotate waist and hip to coordinate with forearm and hit the upper side of ball when it is rising to peak.

④跟随：手臂跟随着身体继续向左前下方随势挥动。

Follow-through：Followed by rotation of body, continue to move arm to the left front downward direction.

⑤还原：松肩沉肘，迅速还原成击球前的准备姿势。

Recovery：Relax shoulder and lower elbow, and recover quickly to the ready position.

**2. 易见错误( misstep)**

步法不到位。
Footwork is wrong.

**3. 纠正( correction)**

判断好来球落点，及时移动。
Make judgment of placement and move in time.

图 3 - 23　横拍正手扣杀

# （九）反手扣杀（Backhand smash）

## 1. 动作特点与运用（characteristics and application）

反手扣杀的特点是动作大、力量重、球速快、落点广，多用于扣杀对手向左半台回击的高球或者半高球。

【动作结构要领】

①选位：根据球的落点调整好站位，身体不宜离球台太近，右脚稍前。

Ready position：According to placement of ball, choose a good ready position with right foot slightly in front. Don't be too close to the table.

②引拍：随着腰、髋向左转动，上臂和前臂引向左侧后方，且引拍至肩，拍面稍前。

Backswing：Rotate waist and hip to left and raise upper arm and forearm to left shoulder high with the racket forward.

③击球：通过重心和手臂的移动，将拍引至来球高度，以及腰和髋的转动与手臂的协调发力，在来球的高点期击球的中上部。

Stroke：Move weight and arm to bring the racket to the height of the coming ball coordinated by rotation of waist, hip and arm. Hit the upper side of the ball.

④跟随：手臂跟随着身体继续向左前下方随势挥动。

Follow-through：Followed by rotation of body, continue to move arm to the left front downward direction.

⑤还原：松肩沉肘，迅速还原成击球前的准备姿势。

Recovery：Relax shoulder and lower elbow, and recover quickly to the ready position.

## 2. 易见错误（misstep）

触球部位与发力方向不对。

Hitting point is wrong and direction of force is wrong.

## 3. 纠正（correction）

触球中上部，向前向下发力。

Hit the upper side of the ball and pull it downward to the front and downward direction.

# （十）正手中远台攻球（Forehand attack off table court）

## 1. 动作特点与运用（characteristics and application）

正手中远台攻球具有站位远、动作幅度大、力量重、步法移动范围较大等特点，多用于远台进攻的相持。

【动作结构要领】（如图 3 - 24、图 3 - 25 所示）

①选位：身体离台约 1 m，两脚开立与肩稍宽，左脚在前。

Ready position：Keep away from the table about 1 m, stand with feet shoulder-width apart or wider, place right foot slightly behind left foot.

②引拍：在髋和腰的带动下向后引拍，动作幅度比正手快攻大，手臂稍抬高。手腕自然放松，拍面前倾。

Backswing：Followed by rotation of waist and hip, raising arm slightly, begin a backswing with larger range of motion than forehand drive. Then relax wrist and lean the racket forward.

③击球：在髋和腰的配合发力下，前臂向前挥拍迎球，在球的下降前期用球拍上半部分击球的中上部。

Stroke：With cooperated force from rotation of hip and waist, move forearm to hit the ball. Hit the upper side of the ball with the upper part of the racket when the ball is beginning to descend.

④跟随：手臂顺势挥拍至头的左侧，重心由右向左。

Follow-through：Move the racket to the left side of head and shift weight from right to left.

⑤还原：松肩沉肘，迅速还原成击球前的准备姿势。

Recovery：Relax shoulder and lower elbow, and recover quickly to the ready position.

## 2. 易见错误（misstep）

引拍幅度小、方向不对。

Backswing is short and direction is wrong.

## 3. 纠正（correction）

加大引拍距离，向后引拍。

Increase more distance of backswing more backward.

图 3 - 24　直拍正手中远台攻球

图 3 - 25　横拍正手中远台攻球

# （十一）反手中远台攻球（Backhand attack off table court）

## 1. 动作特点与运用（characteristics and application）

与正手中远台攻球类似，反手中远台攻球具有站位远、力量重、攻击力强、线路变化多等特点。多用于相持阶段回击落于反手位置的球。

【动作结构要领】

①选位：身体离台约 1 m，两脚开立，比肩稍宽，右脚稍前。

Ready position：Keep away from table about 1 m, stand with feet shoulder-width apart or wider and place left foot slightly behind right foot.

②引拍：髋关节稍往左旋，带动手臂将拍引至身体的左侧后方，手腕内扣，拍面保持前倾。

Backswing：Rotate hip joint to left with racket moving to the left backward side and lay wrist back with racket leaning forward.

③击球：在髋、腰的配合发力下，前臂外旋，向前挥拍迎球，在来球的下降前期，击球的中上部。

Stroke：With coordinated force from rotation of hip and waist, open forearm and move to hit the ball. Hit the upper side of the ball when it is beginning to descend.

④跟随：手臂顺势挥拍至头的右前方，重心由左转向两脚之间。

Follow-through：Move arm to the right-front side of head and shift weight from left foot to middle of feet.

⑤还原：松肩沉肘，迅速还原成击球前的准备姿势。

Recovery：Relax shoulder and lower elbow，and recover quickly to the ready position.

**2. 易见错误( misstep)**

击球时，手臂成直线挥动击球。

Arm is straight to hit the ball.

**3. 纠正( correction)**

体会击球过程中手臂外旋制造弧线的动作。

Understand the action of arm moving outward in the process of stroke.

# (十二)正手杀高球( Forehand smash lob)

**1. 动作特点与运用( characteristics and application)**

正手杀高球又称为正手高压球，其特点是击球点高、动作大、力量重，主要用于进攻在肩以上高度的来球，是还击高球的一种有效方法。

【动作结构要领】( 如图 3 – 26 所示)

①选位：左脚在前，身体离台略远。

Ready position：Keep away from the table with right foot slightly behind left foot.

②引拍：手臂内旋，使拍面前倾，手臂随着腰、髋向右转动，尽量向身体右后方引拍，以增大球拍与来球距离，便于充分发挥击球力量。

Backswing：Lay wrist back with the racket leaning forward followed by rotation of wrist and hip to right and move the racket to the right backward.

③击球：当球跳至头顶高度时，拍面前倾，击球中上部，手臂加速向左前下方挥动，腰、髋同时配合发力。

Stroke：Hit the upper side of the ball with the racket leaning forward when ball is bouncing to head high. With coordinate force from rotation of waist and hip, move arm to the left front-downward direction.

④跟随：手臂继续向前下方挥动，折叠收至左肩前。

Follow-through：Continue to move arm to the front downward direction and fold in front of left shoulder.

⑤还原：松肩沉肘，迅速还原成击球前的准备姿势。

Recovery：Relax shoulder and lower elbow, and recover quickly to the ready position.

**2. 易见错误(misstep)**

击球时机过早。

Timing is too early.

**3. 纠正(correction)**

当来球很高时，应等球稍下降才出手击球。

Hit the ball while it is descending.

图3－26　直拍正手杀高球

## (十三)正手放高球(Forehand lob)

**1. 动作特点与运用(characteristics and application)**

正手放高球是一种防守技术，具有站台远、回球弧线大等特点。往往用于在相持中陷入被动时，为自己回击下一板球争取时间。

【动作结构要领】

①选位：根据来球的线路站位于远台，左脚稍前。

Ready position：Keep away from the table according to the traveling path of ball and place right foot slightly behind left foot.

②引拍：前臂在腰和髋的带动下，将球拍引至身体右后下方。

Backswing：Rotate waist and hip to right to bring the racket to the right backward side of body.

③击球：前臂在上臂的带动下向前上方挥动，拍面稍前倾，在来球的下降期摩擦球的中上部。

Stroke：Followed by action of upper arm, move forearm to the front upward direction with the racket leaning forward. Brush the upper side of the ball when it is descending.

④跟随：击完球后手臂顺势向前上方挥动。

Follow through：Continue to move arm to the front upward direction.

⑤还原：松肩沉肘，迅速还原成击球前的准备姿势。

Recovery：Relax shoulder and lower elbow, and recover quickly to the ready position.

**2. 易见错误(misstep)**

拍面过于后仰，撞击球过多。

The racket is leaned too much and hitting the ball too often.

**3. 纠正(correction)**

击球时拍面稍前倾，摩擦球的中上部。

Lean racket forward to brush the upper side of the ball.

## (十四)正手滑板球(Forehand fake drive)

**1. 动作特点与运用(characteristics and application)**

滑板球是一项辅助进攻技术。它动作小，回球角度大，带有左侧旋(left sidespin)。主要是通过控制手腕来改变拍面方向，调整击球的部位来改变回球线路，运用得好可直接得分。

【动作结构要领】

①选位：选位靠近球台，重心在右脚，左脚在前。

Ready position：Keep close to the table, place weight on right foot and left foot slightly front of right foot.

②引拍：身体略向右转，引拍至身体的右侧前方，拍面稍前倾。

Backswing：Rotate upper body to right slightly, move the racket to the right front and lean the racket forward.

③击球：击球时，手腕外展，在来球的高点期快速摩擦球的中部并向左侧滑动。

Stroke：Open wrist，brush the center of the ball and slide to left when the ball is bouncing to peak.

④跟随：完成击球后球拍继续向右侧前面送出。

Follow-through：Continue to move the racket to the right side after hitting the ball.

⑤还原：松肩沉肘，迅速还原成击球前的准备姿势。

Recovery：Relax shoulder and lower elbow，and recover quickly to the ready position.

### 2. 易见错误（misstep）

击球撞击过多。

Force hitting is too much.

### 3. 纠正（correction）

触球瞬间向左摩擦球。

Brush the left side of the ball.

## （十五）侧身正手攻球（Sideway forehand attack）

### 1. 动作特点与运用（characteristics and application）

侧身正手攻球特点与正手攻球类似，但侧身攻球更具威胁、难度更大、对步法要求更高。结合步法，可以弥补反手进攻能力的不足。

【动作结构要领】（如图 3 - 27、图 3 - 28 所示）

①选位：身体离台大概 40 cm，两脚开立，与肩同宽或稍宽，左脚稍前，两膝微屈，重心压向前脚掌。

Ready position：Keep away from the table about 40 cm, stand with feet shoulder-width apart or wider, place right foot slightly behind left foot and bend knees with weight resting on front part of feet.

②引拍：根据来球线路移动步法，同时侧身向右转腰，引拍至身体后方。

Backswing：Move footwork according to traveling path, and rotate waist to right to bring the racket to the side behind body.

③击球：来球时，迅速蹬地向左转腰，当球在身体的正前方时前臂快速收缩完成击球。

Stroke：Rotate waist to left quickly and pull back forearm quickly to finish the stroke when the ball is in front of body.

④跟随：身体随重心前压，手臂顺势向左前上方挥出。

Follow-through：Move weight to rest on front part of feet and continue to move arm to the left-front direction.

⑤还原：松肩沉肘，迅速还原成击球前的准备姿势。

Recovery：Relax shoulder and lower elbow, and recover quickly to the ready position.

## 2. 易见错误(misstep)

侧身步使用不合理。

Pivot step is wrong.

## 3. 纠正(correction)

根据来球速度的不同、位置和自己攻球方向选择不同的步法。

Choose different footwork according to speed placement and drive direction.

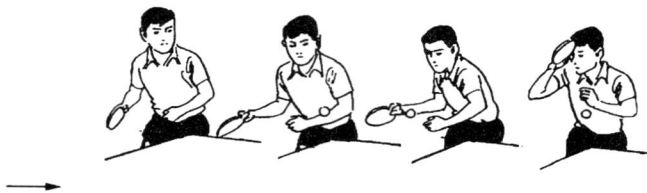

图 3 - 27　直拍侧身正手攻球

图 3 - 28　横拍侧身正手攻球

## （十六）直拍反面攻球（Backhand attack in pen-hold grip）

### 1. 动作特点与运用（characteristics and application）

特点是能增强拍面控制的灵活性，充分发挥前臂的力量。是直拍运动员在相持中常用的技术，也是反手位得分的重要手段。

【动作结构要领】（如图 3－29 所示）

①选位：站位近台，两脚开立与肩稍宽，左脚稍前。

Ready position：Keep close to the table and stand with feet shoulder-width apart or wider and left foot slightly in front.

②引拍：含胸收腹，重心稍低，前臂手腕内收，引拍至腹前。

Backswing：Pull stomach in, lower weight, lay back arm and wrist and move racket to front of abdomen.

③击球：击球时拍面前倾，触球瞬间手腕外展，在来球的上升期击球的中上部。

图 3－29　直拍反面攻球

Stroke：Lean forward the racket, open wrist when contact, and hit the upper side of the ball while it is rising.

④跟随：前臂顺势向前上方发力。

Follow-through：Continue to move forearm to the front upward direction.

⑤还原：迅速还原成击球前的准备姿势。

Recovery：Relax shoulder and lower elbow, and recover quickly to the ready position.

### 2. 易见错误（misstep）

击球时手腕和小臂过于僵硬。

Wrist and forearm are too tight.

### 3. 纠正(correction)

松肩沉肘,手腕后屈内旋。

Relax shoulder, lower elbow and lay wrist back.

# 六、搓球技术(The techniques of push)

搓球是近台回击下旋球的一种基本技术。按搓球的时机,可分为慢搓和快搓;按搓球的旋转性质,可分为搓转与不转和搓侧旋球;按搓球的落点,可分为搓长球和搓短球。动作技术特点是动作小、弧线低、落点活、旋转变化多等。可以牵制对方的进攻,并为抢攻创造机会。

## (一)慢搓(Slow push)

### 1. 动作特点与运用(characteristics and application)

具有动作幅度较大、回球速度较慢、稳定性强的特点。适用于回接旋转较强(heavy spin),线路较长的来球。如与快搓结合,能变化击球的节奏。

(1)正手慢搓(forehand slow push)

【动作结构要领】(如图 3 - 30 所示)

①选位:右脚稍前,站位近台。

Ready position:Keep close to the table with right foot slightly in front.

②引拍:前臂和手腕外旋使拍面稍后仰,身体略向右转,向右上方引拍。

Backswing:Open forearm and wrist with racket leaning backward slightly, rotate upper body to right slightly and move the racket to the left upward.

③击球:在来球的下降前期用球拍摩擦球的中下部,前臂加速向前下方用力的同时手腕内旋配合用力。

Stroke:Brush the bottom of the ball when the ball is descending. Snap forearm and wrist to make maximum acceleration downward.

④跟随:前臂随势前送。

Follow-through:Continue to move forearm.

⑤还原:松肩沉肘,迅速还原成击球前的准备姿势。

Recovery:Relax shoulder and lower elbow, and recover quickly to the ready position.

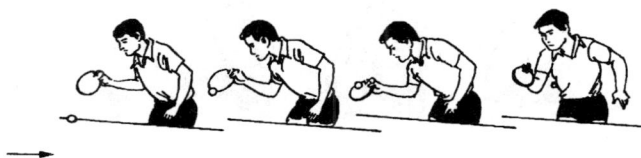

图 3 - 30　直拍正手慢搓

（2）反手慢搓（backhand slowly push）

【动作结构要领】（如图 3 - 31、图 3 - 32 所示）

①选位：站位近台，右脚稍前。

Ready position：Keep close to the table with left foot slightly behind right foot.

②引拍：前臂和手腕内旋使拍引至腹前，拍面稍后仰，身体略向右转，向右上方引拍。

Backswing：Lay back forearm and wrist，bring the racket in front of abdomen，lean the racket forward，rotate body to right slightly and bring the racket to the right front.

③击球：在来球的下降前期用球拍摩擦球的中下部，前臂加速向前下方用力的同时手腕内旋配合用力。

Stroke：Brush the bottom of the ball when the ball is descending. Snap forearm and wrist to make maximum acceleration downward.

④跟随：前臂随势前送。

Follow-through：Continue to move forearm.

⑤还原：松肩沉肘，迅速还原成击球前的准备姿势。

Recovery：Relax shoulder and lower elbow，and recover quickly to the ready position.

## 2. 易见错误（misstep）

击球时机过早，控制不好回球落点。

Contact timing is too early. Control of placement is poor.

## 3. 纠正（correction）

在来球下降前期击球。

Hit the ball while it is descending.

图 3 – 31　直拍反手慢搓

图 3 – 32　横拍反手慢搓

# （二）快搓（Fast push）

## 1. 动作特点与运用（characteristics and application）

具有击球动作幅度小、回球速度快、弧线低，借助对方来球的前冲力进攻的特点。常用于接发球或削过来的近网下旋球。快搓与其他搓球技术相结合能改变击球的节奏，缩短对方准备击球的时间，为争取主动创造条件。

（1）正手快搓（forehand fast push）

【动作结构要领】

①选位：右脚稍前，站位近台。

Ready position：Keep close to the table with right foot slightly in front.

②引拍：前臂外旋向后上方提起，后引动作较小。

Backswing：Open forearm, lift the racket to the up backward direction with a short backswing.

③击球：击球时拍面稍后仰，前臂前伸迎球，在来球的上升期击球中下部借对方来球的冲力，前臂、手腕适当用力向前下方挥动。

Stroke：Push forearm forward to opponent's return with racket leaning backward. Snap forearm and wrist slightly to hit the bottom of the ball and move downward when the ball is rising.

④跟随：前臂随势前送，幅度较小。

Follow-through：Continue to move forearm with a small range of action.

⑤还原：松肩沉肘，迅速还原成击球前的准备姿势。

Recovery：Relax shoulder and lower elbow, and recover quickly to the ready position.

（2）反手快搓（backhand fast push）

【动作结构要领】（如图 3－33、图 3－34 所示）

图 3－33　直拍反手快搓

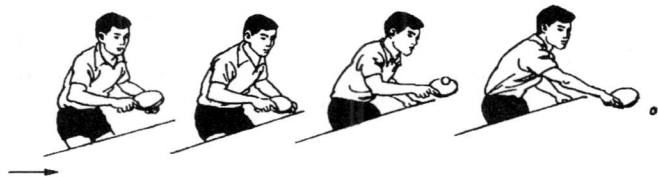

图 3－34　横拍反手快搓

①选位：右脚稍前，站位近台。

Ready position：Keep close to the table with right foot slightly in front.

②引拍：手臂自然弯曲，手腕适当放松，球拍往后引至腹前。

Backswing：Bend arm naturally with wrist relaxed, move racket to the front of abdomen.

③击球：击球时，拍面稍后仰，在来球的上升期击球中下部，借对方来球的冲力，前臂、手腕适当用力向前下方挥动。

Stroke：Lean the racket backward and hit the bottom of the ball when it is bouncing. With force bringing from opponent, move forearm and wrist to the front down direction with medium force.

④跟随：前臂随势前送，幅度较小。

Follow-through：Continue to move forearm with a small range of action.

⑤还原：松肩沉肘，迅速还原成击球前的准备姿势。

Recovery：Relax shoulder and lower elbow，and recover quickly to the ready position.

## 2. 易见错误(misstep)

击球时机过晚，回球速度慢。

Timing is too late，and returning speed is slow.

## 3. 纠正(correction)

在来球的上升期击球。

Hit the ball while it is rising.

# (三)搓转与不转(Spin or non-spin push)

## 1. 动作特点与运用(characteristics and application)

用相似的手法搓出转与不转两种旋转的球来迷惑对方。与其他搓球技术结合使用，是选手争取主动的过渡手段，也是组成搓攻技术的主要内容，具有旋转强度差异大的特点。

【动作结构要领】

①选位：右脚稍前，站位近台。

Ready position：Keep close to the table with right foot slightly in front.

②引拍：手臂自然弯曲，手腕适当放松，拍后引至腹前。

Backswing：Bend arm naturally with wrist relaxed，and move racket to the abdomen.

③击球：拍面稍后仰，在来球的上升期击球中下部，前臂、手腕加速向前下方切球。

Stroke：Racket leans backward. With a short downward movement of forearm and wrist，hit the bottom of the ball when it is rising.

④跟随：前臂随势前送。

Follow-through：Continue to move arm forward.

⑤还原：松肩沉肘，迅速还原成击球前的准备姿势。

Recovery：Relax shoulder and lower elbow，and recover quickly to the ready position.

搓不转球动作结构与搓转球动作结构基本一致，主要区别在于击球时用球拍的上半部或中部撞击球。

## 2. 易见错误（misstep）

击球点选择错误。

Contact point is wrong.

## 3. 纠正（correction）

当来球旋转强时，搓球的下部；旋转弱时，搓球的中部偏下。

If the ball is with heavy spin, push bottom part of the ball; if it is light spin, push the ball downward.

# （四）搓侧旋球（Sidespin push ）

## 1. 动作特点与运用（characteristics and application）

具有动作小，速度快，旋转变化大的特点。在接发球或对搓过渡中，运用正反手搓侧旋，使回击过去的球向两侧拐弯，能减弱对方的攻势或使对方的回球弧线过高，为抢攻创造条件。

（1）正手搓左侧旋球（forehand sidespin push ）

【动作结构要领】

①选位：右脚稍前，站位近台。

Ready position：Keep close to the table with right foot slightly in front.

②引拍：大臂略提起，前臂稍外展向右前方引拍。

Backswing：Lift upper arm slightly, lean forearm forward with racket moving to the right front.

③击球：在高点期或下降前期手臂向左侧挥动发力，同时手腕稍内旋辅助发力。

Stroke：Lay wrist back slightly while moving forearm to left side, when the ball is beginning to descend.

④跟随：前臂随势前送。

Follow-through：Continue to move arm forward.

⑤还原：松肩沉肘，迅速还原成击球前的准备姿势。

Recovery：Relax shoulder and lower elbow, and recover quickly to the ready position.

（2）正手搓右侧旋球（forehand right sidespin push）

【动作结构要领】

①选位：右脚稍前，站位近台。

Ready position：Keep close to the table with right foot slightly in front.

②引拍：手臂自然弯曲，略向左后方引拍，手腕稍内旋，拍面后仰。

Backswing：Bend arm naturally with wrist relaxed, move the racket to the left backward backswing and lay wrist back with racket leaning backward.

③击球：在高点期或下降前期手臂向右侧挥动发力，同时手腕稍内旋辅助发力。

Stroke：Move forearm to right and wrist toward inside when the ball is beginning to descend.

④跟随：前臂随势前送。

Follow-through：Continue to move arm forward.

⑤还原：松肩沉肘，迅速还原成击球前的准备姿势。

Recovery：Relax shoulder and lower elbow, and recover quickly to the ready position.

**2. 易见错误(misstep)**

击球时拍面角度控制错误。

Racket angle is wrong.

**3. 纠正(correction)**

拍面稍后仰触球的中上部。

Lean the racket backward to hit the upper side of the ball.

# (五)搓球摆短(Drop shot push)

**1. 动作特点与运用(characteristics and application)**

具有动作幅度小、出手快、回球短的特点，是下旋球和接发球的有效控制技术。

(1)正手搓球摆短(forehand drop shot push)

【动作结构要领】(如图3-35所示)

①选位：右脚稍前，站位近台。

Ready position：Keep close to the table with right foot slightly in front.

②引拍：拍面稍后仰，向右侧后方引拍。

Backswing：Lean the racket backward and move to the right backward.

③击球：在高点期或下降前期手臂向右侧挥动发力，同时手腕稍内旋辅助发力。

Stroke：Move arm to right and wrist toward inside when the ball is beginning to descend.

④跟随：前臂随势前送，幅度较小。

Follow-through：Continue to move forearm with a small range of action.

⑤还原：松肩沉肘，迅速还原成击球前的准备姿势。

Recovery：Relax shoulder and lower elbow, and recover quickly to the ready position.

图 3 – 35 正手搓球摆短

（2）反手搓球摆短（backhand drop shot push）

【动作结构要领】

①选位：右脚稍前，站位近台。

Ready position：Keep close to the table with right foot slightly in front.

②引拍：拍面稍后仰，向左侧后方引拍。

Backswing：Lean the racket backward and move to the left backward.

③击球：在来球的上升期击球的中下部，前臂向前下方挥动，同时手腕适当外展发力。

Stroke：Move wrist to the front downward direction while waving forearm to downside in front of your body when the ball is rising.

④跟随：前臂随势前送，幅度较小。

Follow-through：Continue to move forearm with small range of action.

⑤还原：松肩沉肘，迅速还原成击球前的准备姿势。

Recovery：Relax shoulder and lower elbow, and recover quickly to the ready position.

**2. 易见错误(misstep)**

握拍太紧不够放松，致使回球过长过高。

Tight grip leads to high return.

**3. 纠正(correction)**

触球瞬间手腕放松，根据球旋转强弱调整拍形。

Relax wrist to adjust racket angle based on amount of spin while hitting the ball.

## (六)正手削球(Forehand chop)

**1. 动作特点与运用(characteristics and application)**

正手削球一般用来处理球台右半台的下旋球，具有稳定性好的特点，可以为进攻创造机会。

【动作结构要领】(如图 3－36、图 3－37 所示)

①选位：右脚稍后，身体略向右转。

Ready position：Stand with feet apart and right foot slightly behind and rotate body to right slightly.

②引拍：拍面基本与台面垂直，向右后方引拍至肩高。

Backswing：Keep the racket vertical with the table, and move the racket to right behind body to the height of shoulder.

③击球：在来球的下降前期，前臂在上臂的带动下，随身体重心的移动向左前下方挥动，摩擦球的中下部。

Stroke：Followed by rotation of weight, move forearm to the left front downward direction. Brush the bottom of the ball while it is beginning to descend.

④跟随：前臂顺势向左前下方挥出。

Follow-through：Continue to move forearm to the left front downward direction.

⑤还原：迅速还原成击球前的准备姿势。

Recovery：Recover quickly to the ready position.

**2. 易见错误(misstep)**

不是前臂带动上臂向上引拍，而是用肘部直接向后拉。

Forearm does not bring upper arm upward. Just the elbow moves directly backward.

## 3. 纠正（correction）

强调前臂带动上臂向上引拍。

Pay attention to forearm to bring upper arm to upward.

图 3－36　直拍正手削球

图 3－37　横拍正手削球

# （七）反手削球（Backhand chop）

## 1. 动作特点与运用（characteristics and application）

多用来处理左半台与中台的下旋球，与正手削球相同，具有稳定性好的特点，可以限制对手的进攻和为自己创造进攻机会。

【动作结构要领】（如图 3－38、图 3－39 所示）

①选位：左脚稍后，身体略向左转。

Ready position：Stand with left foot slightly behind, and rotate body to left slightly.

②引拍：拍面基本与台面垂直，向左后方引拍至肩高附近。

Backswing：Keep the racket face vertical with the table and move to the left backward backswing which is shoulder high.

③击球：前臂在上臂的带动下，随身体重心向右前下方挥动，在球的下降前期摩擦球的中下部。

Stroke：Followed by rotation of weight, move forearm to the right front downward direction. Brush the bottom of the ball while it is beginning to descend.

图 3－38　直拍反手削球

图 3－39　横拍反手削球

④跟随：前臂顺势向左前下方挥出。

Follow-through：Continue to move forearm to the left front downward direction.

⑤还原：迅速还原成击球前的准备姿势。

Recovery：Recover quickly to the ready position.

## 2. 易见错误（misstep）

拍形过于后仰，削强烈下旋或弧圈球时容易回击高球。

The racket is open too much. Chop heavy backspin or loop with high traveling path.

## 3. 纠正（correction）

强调引拍时拍面应稍竖立。

The racket should stand vertically while doing backswing.

# 七、拉球技术（The techniques of topspin stroke）

拉球是一种攻击力强，威力大的进攻技术。而其中又以弧圈球（loop）技术为代表。弧圈球技术可分为正手弧圈球和反手弧圈球。根据弧圈球技术的旋转特征可分为加转弧圈球（heavy loop）、前冲弧圈球和侧旋弧圈球。下面介绍几种主要拉球技术。

## （一）正手快拉（Forehand fast topspin stroke）

### 1. 动作特点与运用（characteristics and application）

正手快拉也可称为正手拉抽或拉攻，具有速度较快、动作较小、线路较灵活等特点。在比赛中，用正手提拉出各种不同落点和轻重力量相结合的上旋球，伺机进行突击或扣杀，是一项对付削球（chop）打法的重要技术。

【动作结构要领】（如图 3 - 40、图 3 - 41 所示）

①选位：站位近台，左脚稍前。

Ready position：Keep close to the table with left foot slightly in front.

②引拍：向后下方引拍的同时转腰、沉肩，重心在右脚上。

Backswing：Rotate waist to right, lower right shoulder, bring racket to the back downward backswing and rest weight on right foot.

③击球：拍面稍前倾，在来球的高点期或下降前期击球的中部或中上部。

Stroke：Lean the racket forward slightly, and hit the center or upper side of the ball when it is peak or beginning to descend.

④跟随：随势挥拍。

Follow-through：Racket continue to move the racket.

⑤还原：松肩沉肘，迅速还原成击球前的准备姿势。

Recovery：Relax shoulder and lower elbow, and recover quickly to the ready position.

**2. 易见错误 ( misstep )**

击球时机过晚。

Timing is too late.

**3. 纠正 ( correction )**

在来球的高点期或下降前期击球。

Hit the ball when it is beginning to descend.

图 3 - 40    直拍正手拉球

图 3 - 41    横拍正手拉球

# （二）反手快拉 ( Backhand fast topspin stroke )

### 1. 动作特点与运用 ( characteristics and application )

反手快拉也称反手快抽或快攻，具有站位近、动作小、速度较快、落点变化多等特点。是横拍 ( shake-hand grip ) 选手对付下旋来球的一项重要技术，也是近年来进攻型选手为加强反手位的进攻，用反手背面快拉的一种新技术。

【动作结构要领】( 如图 3 - 42 所示 )

①选位：两脚平行，站位近台。

Ready position：Keep close to the table. Feet are parallel.

②引拍：向后下方引拍的同时转腰、沉肩，重心在右脚上。

Backswing：Rotate waist to right，lower right shoulder，bring racket to the back downward and rest weight on right foot.

③击球：拍面稍前倾，在来球的高点期或下降前期击球的中部或中上部。

Stroke：Racket face lean forward slightly，and hit the center or upper side of the ball when it is beginning to descend.

④跟随：随势挥拍。

Follow-through：Continue to move the racket.

⑤还原：松肩沉肘，迅速还原成击球前的准备姿势。

Recovery：Relax shoulder and lower elbow，and recover quickly to the ready position.

### 2. 易见错误（misstep）

击球时机过晚。

Timing is too late.

### 3. 纠正（correction）

在来球的高点期或下降前期击球。

Hit the ball when it is beginning to descend.

图 3-42　横拍反手快拉

## （三）拉加转弧圈球（Heavy loop）

### 1. 动作特点与运用（characteristics and application）

具有飞行弧线较高，球速较慢，上旋强的特点。球着台后下滑速度较快，击出的球第一弧线较高，第二弧线较低，是对付下旋球（backspin）的有效技术。在相持中，可以对击球节奏进行变化。

（1）正手拉加转弧圈球（forehand heavy loop）

【动作结构要领】（如图3 –43、图3 –44所示）

图3 –43　直拍正手拉加转弧圈球

图3 –44　横拍正手拉加转弧圈球

①选位：左脚稍前，两膝微屈。

Ready position：Place left foot slightly in front and bend knees.

②引拍：手臂自然下垂，向右后下方引拍，身体随之向右转动，右肩下沉，重心落在右脚上。

Backswing：Drop arm naturally，bring racket to the right backward rotate upper body to right with a low right shoulder and rest weight on right foot.

③击球：在来球的下降前期击球的中部或中上部，在摩擦球的瞬间迅速收缩前臂加大摩擦力。

Stroke：Hit the center or upper side of the ball when it is beginning to descend and snap the front arm to make maximum friction.

④跟随：随势挥拍至头部高度。

Follow-through：Continue to move the racket to the height of head.

⑤还原：松肩沉肘，迅速还原成击球前的准备姿势。

Recovery：Relax shoulder and lower elbow, and recover quickly to the ready position.

（2）反手拉加转弧圈球（backhand heavy loop）

【动作结构要领】（如图 3 - 45 所示）

图 3 - 45　反手拉加转弧圈球

①选位：两脚平行或右脚稍前。

Ready position：Stand with feet parallel or right foot slightly in front.

②引拍：两膝微屈，重心在两脚间，右肩下沉，球拍引至腹前下方。

Backswing：Bend knees with weight resting on middle of feet, lower right shoulder and bring racket to the front downward direction of abdomen.

③击球：手腕内旋，拍面稍前倾，在来球的下降前期用力摩擦球的中上部。

Stroke：Lay back wrist, lean the racket forward slightly, and brush the upper side of the ball when it is descending.

④跟随：前臂随势前送。

Follow-through：Continue to move the racket to the height of head.

⑤还原：松肩沉肘，迅速还原成击球前的准备姿势。

Recovery：Relax shoulder and lower elbow, and recover quickly to the ready position.

**2. 易见错误(misstep)**

(1)引拍不够。

Backswing is not enough.

(2)击球时机把握不好。

Timing is wrong.

**3. 纠正(correction)**

(1)手臂自然下垂向右后下方引拍，右肩下沉，重心在右脚上。

Drop arm naturally and move to the right down backward and lower right shoulder with weight resting on right foot.

(2)在来球的下降前期用力摩擦球的中上部。

Brush the upper side of the ball while it is descending.

## (四)拉前冲弧圈球 (Drive accelerated loop)

**1. 动作特点与运用(characteristics and application)**

具有出手快，球速快，弧线低，上旋强，着台后前冲力大等特点。它是一种将力量和旋转结合得较好的进攻性技术，也是对付发球(serve)、搓球(push)、削球(chop)、推挡(block)以及在相持中对拉(counter topspin)的有效技术。

(1)正手拉前冲弧圈球 (forehand accelerated loop)

【动作结构要领】(如图3-46、图3-47所示)

①选位：左脚稍前，两膝微屈。

Ready position：Place left foot slightly in front and bend knees.

②引拍：腰向右转动，重心移至右脚向右后方引拍。

Backswing：Rotate waist to right, shift weight to right foot and move the racket to the right backward.

③击球：击球时拍面前倾，在上臂带动下前臂加速向前上方挥动，手腕配合发力，在来球的上升后期或高点期摩擦球的中上部。

Stroke：Followed by upper arm, snap forearm and wrist to the front upward

图 3 - 46　直拍正手拉前冲弧圈球

图 3 - 47　横拍正手拉前冲弧圈球

direction, and lean the racket forward. Brush the upper side of the ball when it is bouncing to peak.

④跟随：随势挥拍至头部高度。

Follow-through: Continue to move the racket to the height of head.

⑤还原：松肩沉肘，迅速还原成击球前的准备姿势。

Recovery: Relax shoulder and lower elbow, and recover quickly to the ready position.

(2)反手拉前冲弧圈球(backhand accelerated loop)

【动作结构要领】

①选位：两脚平行或右脚稍前。

Ready position: Stand with feet parallel or right foot slightly in front.

②引拍：两膝微屈，重心在两脚间。右肩下沉，球拍引至大腿内侧。

Backswing: Bend knees with weight resting on middle of feet, lower right shoulder and bring racket to the left side of leg.

③击球：击球时拍面稍前倾，以肘关节为轴，前臂快速向前上方发力，在来球的高点期摩擦球的中上部。

Stroke: Lean the racket forward slightly, pivot forearm around elbow and snap to the front upward direction, and brush the upper side of the ball when it is on peak.

④跟随：前臂随势前送。

Follow-through：Continue to move the racket to head high.

⑤还原：松肩沉肘，迅速还原成击球前的准备姿势。

Recovery：Relax shoulder and lower elbow, and recover quickly to the ready position.

**2. 易见错误(misstep)**

(1)重心转移不够。

Rotation of weight is not enough.

(2)击球时机把握不好。

Timing is wrong.

**3. 纠正(correction)**

(1)蹬腿转腰，重心从右脚转至左脚。

Straighten leg and then rotate waist to shift weight from right foot to left foot.

(2)在来球的下降前期用力摩擦球的中上部。

Brush the upper side of the ball while it is beginning to descend.

# (五)正手拉侧旋弧圈球(Forehand sidespin loop)

## 1. 动作特点与运用(characteristics and application)

具有飞行弧线向侧偏拐、强烈的侧上旋、着台后急速向侧下滑落的特点。多用于处理正手拉大角度的来球。

【动作结构要领】(如图3－48、图3－49所示)

①选位：左脚稍前，两膝微屈。

Ready position：Place left foot slightly in front and bend knees.

②引拍：重心在右脚上，球拍引至身体的右侧后方。

Backswing：Rest weight on right foot, bring the racket to the right backward side of body.

③击球：腰向左转，上臂带动前臂迅速挥动，在来球的下降前期摩擦球的右侧中部或下部，向外侧并向前上方挥拍。

Stroke：Rotate waist to left, snap forearm and brush the right-center or bottom of the ball when it is descending.

④跟随：随势挥拍至头部高度。

Follow-through：Continue to move the racket the height of head.

⑤还原：松肩沉肘，迅速还原成击球前的准备姿势。

Recovery：Relax shoulder and lower elbow, and recover quickly to the ready position.

图 3-48　直拍正手拉右侧弧圈球

图 3-49　横拍正手拉右侧弧圈球

## 2. 易见错误（misstep）

击球点选择不对。

Contact point is wrong.

## 3. 纠正（correction）

摩擦球的右侧中部或下部向外侧。

Brush the right-center or bottom of the ball.

# （六）正手反拉弧圈球（Forehand topspin stroke against loop）

## 1. 动作特点与运用（characteristics and application）

正手反拉弧圈球是一项难度较高的技术，可以在相持环节中抓住机会反拉对方的弧圈球，是由防守转为进攻的重要技术。

【动作结构要领】

①选位：双脚平行或左脚稍前。

Ready position：Stand with feet parallel or left foot slightly in front.

②引拍：腰向右转动，向右后方引拍，重心移至右脚。

Backswing：Rotate waist to right，bring racket to the right backward，and rest weight on right foot.

③击球：击球时拍面前倾，在上臂带动下前臂加速向前上方挥动，手腕配合发力，在来球的上升后期击球。

Stroke：Lean the racket forward，snap forearm and wrist upward and hit the ball when it is rising to peak.

④跟随：随势挥拍至头部高度。

Follow-through：Continue to move the racket to the height of head.

⑤还原：松肩沉肘，迅速还原成击球前的准备姿势。

Recovery：Relax shoulder and lower elbow，and recover quickly to the ready position.

## 2. 易见错误（misstep）

动作幅度过大。

Movement range is too large.

**3. 纠正（correction）**

动作紧凑，通过小幅度转腰，身体迎前击球。

Rotate waist in small range to return.

## （七）反手反撕弧圈球（Backhand force brush against loop）

**1. 动作特点与运用（characteristics and application）**

反手反撕弧圈球是一项具有进攻性的反手技术，无论是进攻还是防守都有一定威胁性，有利于在比赛中争取积极主动。

【动作结构要领】

①选位：双脚平行或左脚稍前。

Ready position：Stand with feet parallel or left foot slightly in front.

②引拍：右肩下沉，引拍时位置稍高，手腕略微内收，保持拍形。

Backswing：Lower right shoulder，place racket in a slightly high backswing and lay wrist back slightly to fix racket angle.

③击球：球拍稍前倾迎球，上升期借来球的力量，在接触球瞬间自下向上转带拍头，增强对球的摩擦出球。

Stroke：Lean the racket forward slightly，hit the ball while it is rising and brush the ball with more friction from downward to upward.

④跟随：随势挥拍。

Follow-through：Continue to move the racket.

⑤还原：松肩沉肘，迅速还原成击球前的准备姿势。

Recovery：Relax shoulder and lower elbow，and recover quickly to the ready position.

**2. 易见错误（misstep）**

引拍不够。

Backswing is not enough.

**3. 纠正（correction）**

向后引拍时球拍保持在较高位置，可以在接触球时更容易调整击球的角度。

Keep racket in a high position and adjust racket angle while hitting the ball.

# （八）直拍反手拉弧圈球（Reverse backhand loop in pen-hold grip）

## 1. 动作特点与运用（characteristics and application）

直拍反面拉弧圈球具有回球速度快、侧拐度大、弧线低、威胁性大等特点。在对方不适应此种旋转或节奏变化时，往往能直接得分。

【动作结构要领】

①选位：站位近台，两脚开立与肩同宽或稍宽，左脚稍前。

Ready position：Keep close to the table. Stand with feet shoulder-width apart or wider and left foot slightly in front.

②引拍：两膝微屈，身体略向右旋，拍面前倾，放松手腕和手臂引拍。

Backswing：Bend knees and rotate body to right, lean the racket forward, and relax wrist and arm.

③击球：蹬地转腰，带动手臂前上方挥出，在来球的高点期摩擦球的中上部。

Stroke：Rotate waist, move racket to the front upward direction and brush the upper side of the ball when it is rising to peak.

④跟随：手臂向斜上方顺势挥出。

Follow-through：Continue to move arm.

⑤还原：松肩沉肘，迅速还原成击球前的准备姿势。

Recovery：Relax shoulder and lower elbow, and recover quickly to the ready position.

## 2. 易见错误（misstep）

挥臂没有弧线，球容易下网。

There is no trajectory in movement of arm, so the ball is easy to be blocked by net.

## 3. 纠正（correction）

手臂应该有弧线地向前上方挥出。

Arm should be moved to the front and upward direction in trajectory.

# (九)反手拧拉(Reverse backhand twist topspin stroke)

## 1. 动作特点与运用(characteristics and application)

反手拧拉时摩擦球比较充分,容易克服来球的旋转,使得回球稳定性好并且带有强烈的旋转,从而在接发球过程中变被动为主动。

【动作结构要领】(如图3-50所示)

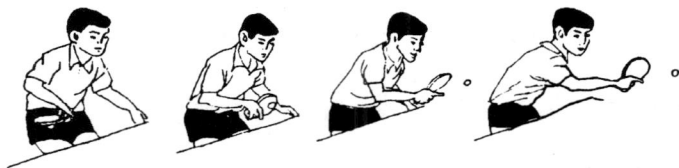

图3-50 横拍反手拧拉

①选位:根据来球调整步伐,右脚上步并将重心调整至右脚后撤步,同时左脚向后撤步,身体大致与球台端线平行。

Ready position:Adjust footwork according to the traveling path of the ball and keep body almost parallel to the end line of the table.

②引拍:身体前倾,降低重心,腹部内收,手臂在击球前保持一定的稳定性,手腕大幅度内收并确保球拍与球台近似水平状态。

Backswing:Lean body forward with weight in a low position and pull stomach in. Keep arm in a steady way before hitting the ball, and lay back wrist in a large margin to make sure that racket is parallel to table approximately.

③击球:在来球的上升期或者最高点,小臂以胳膊肘为轴心向右前方展开并将手腕打开,摩擦球的中上部。为了方便发力,应调整步伐与手臂在胸部的正前方完成击球。

Stroke:Pivot forearm around elbow with wrist open to brush the upper side of the ball when it is rising. Footwork and arm should be adjusted to make sure hitting is finished in front of chest.

④跟随:小臂与手腕顺势向右前方外展。

Follow-through:Continue to move arm and wrist to the right front direction.

⑤还原:松肩沉肘,迅速还原成击球前的准备姿势。

Recovery: Relax shoulder and lower elbow, and recover quickly to the ready position.

### 2. 易见错误(misstep)

挥拍时，大臂用力过多。
Snap upper arm too much.

### 3. 纠正(correction)

以小臂发力为主，从而提高回球的稳定性。
Mainforce is from forearm to increase stability of return.

# 八、步法(Footworks)

乒乓球步法是指击球者在移动过程中依靠下肢完成的各种动作。主要包括单步(one step)、并步(side step)、侧身步(sideway step)、交叉步(cross step)等，有时需要将其中两种或两种以上步法结合起来使用。练就启动快、移动到位的步法，能保持合适的击球位置，提高动作质量，又能扩大控制球的范围。

## (一)单步(One step)

### 1. 移动方法(moving methods)

以一只脚为轴，另一只脚向前、后、左、右不同方向移动，身体重心随之落在移动脚上。(如图3-51所示)
Pivot around one foot as axis while another one moves to the front direction or the backward direction or the left direction or the right direction and rest weight on the moving foot.

### 2. 运用时机(application timing)

接近网小球(ball near to net)；削追身球(chop body-hit)。单步侧身攻球在位于中线稍偏左的来球落点(placement)或对推侧身突击直线或对搓中提拉球时常用。

## ( 二 ) 并步 ( Side step )

### 1. 移动方法 ( moving methods )

一脚先向另一脚并半步或一小步, 另一脚在并步脚落地后随即向来球方向移动一步。( 如图 3 - 52 所示 )

Slide one foot close to another foot and then step to the ball.

### 2. 运用时机 ( application timing )

快攻选手 ( fast-driver ) 在左右移动中攻或拉球; 削球选手正反手削球。并步侧身攻 ( sideway step ), 多用于拉削球 ( topspin stroke against chop ), 右脚先向左脚后并一步, 以便转体 ( rotate body ), 随之左脚向侧跨一步。

图 3 - 51　单步

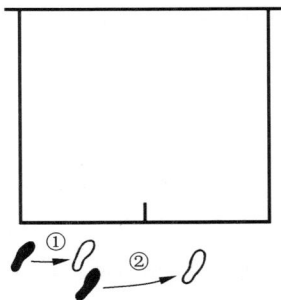

图 3 - 52　并步

## ( 三 ) 交叉步 ( Cross step )

### 1. 移动方法 ( moving methods )

以靠近来球方向的脚作为支撑脚, 该脚的脚尖调整指向移动方向, 远离来球方向的脚在体前交叉, 向来球方向跨出一大步, 身体随之向来球方向转动, 支撑脚跟着向来球方向再迈一步, 这是前交叉步。后交叉步是在体后完成交叉动作。( 如图 3 - 53、图 3 - 54 所示 )

Begin the cross step by taking a wide step with the right leg. Step across with the left leg in front of the right leg and strike the ball. At the end of the stroke, finish right leg in a wide position to allow you to push back to the left.

**2. 运用时机（application timing）**

快攻或弧圈打法在侧身攻、拉后扑打右角空当（empty）；从右大角变反手击球；在走动中拉削球；削球打法接短球（chopper returns ball near net）或削突击球（chop against sudden drive）。

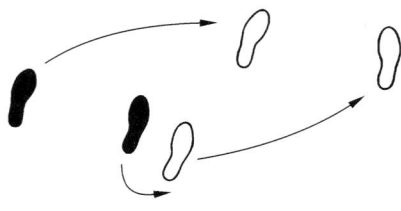

图3-53　前交叉步

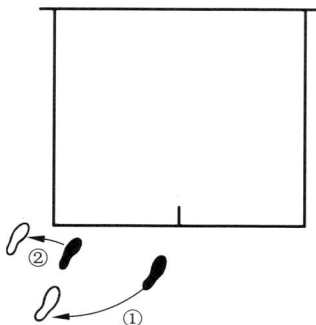

图3-54　后交叉步

## （四）侧身步（Sideway step）

**1. 移动方法（moving methods）**

左脚向左侧跨一步，右脚向左侧后方移动，同时上体收腹侧转腰，重心落在右脚上。（如图3-55所示）

Take a large step of left foot to left, then move right foot back to left, rotate upper body to right and rest weight on right foot.

**2. 运用时机（application timing）**

多用于拉削球（topspin stroke against chop）；抢攻反手位的来球。

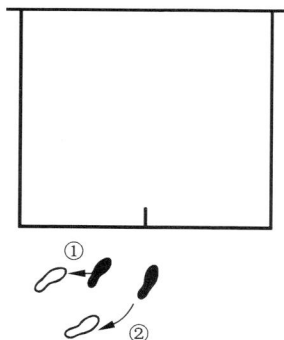

图3-55　侧身步

# 第四章 乒乓球的基本战术
## (Basic tactics of table tennis)

## 一、推攻战术 (Block and attack tactics)

### (一)特点(Characteristics)

主要运用正手攻球(forehand attack)和反手推挡(backhand block)的速度和力量以及结合落点变化和节奏变化来压制、调动对方,以争取主动并得分。推攻战术是用左推右攻打法(backhand block with forehand attack)对付攻击型打法(offensive play)的主要战术,有反手推挡能力的两面攻运动员、攻削结合运动员(attacking chopper)等也常使用它。

### (二)方法(Methods)

(1)左推右攻(Backhand block with forehand attack)。

(2)推挡侧身攻(Sideway attack after block)。

(3)推挡侧身攻后扑正手(Sideway attack after block, and then rush to one's forehand with drive)。

(4)左推结合反手攻(Backhand block with backhand attack)。

(5)左推、反手攻、侧身攻后扑正手(Backhand block with backhand attack, sideway attack, and then rush at one's forehand with drive)。

### (三)注意事项(Precautions)

(1)推、攻都要有线路变化、落点(placement)变化和节奏变化,这是推攻战术争取主动和创造扣杀(smash)机会的主要方法。

(2)推挡一般以压对方反手为主,然后突然变正手,以创造进攻机会。如果对方正手(forehand)较差,才可用以推对方正手为主。

(3)在推挡(block)中突然加力推(force block)对方中路,使对方难于用力回击,然后用正手或侧身扣杀。

（4）遇到机会球时要果断扣杀，这是推攻战术得分的主要手段。

（5）推攻战术要坚持近台（close-to-table），但不能死守近台，要学会近台和中台的位置转换，掌握比赛节奏。

（6）推攻战术对付弧圈类打法应坚持以近台为主，用快推和加、减力推挡（cushion block）来控制落点，伺机采用近台反拉或中等力量扣杀弧圈球，然后进入正手连续进攻（continuous forehand attack）。

## 二、拉攻战术（Topspin stroke and attack tactics）

### （一）特点（Characteristics）

连续运用正手快拉创造进攻机会，然后采用突击（make a sudden and violent attack）和扣杀（smash）来作为得分手段。拉攻战术是快攻打法应对削球类打法的主要战术。

### （二）方法（Methods）

（1）正手拉后扣杀（smash after forehand topspin stroke）。
（2）反手拉后扣杀（smash after backhand topspin stroke）。

### （三）注意事项（Precautions）

（1）拉、扣的力量要有较大悬殊，使对方措手不及。

（2）拉球（topspin stroke）要有线路（line）和落点变化以调动对方，争取创造主动进攻机会。

（3）遇到机会球时要大胆扣杀（smash）或突击（make a sudden and violent drive）。

（4）采用拉攻战术要有耐心，不能急于求成，对没有把握的球不要过凶。

## 三、搓攻战术（Push stroke and attack tactics）

### （一）特点（Characteristics）

主要运用"转、低、快、变"（spin, low, speed, variation）的搓球控制对方，以寻找战机，然后采用突击、快点（flip）或拉攻（topspin stroke）等技术展开攻势并进入连续进攻。在搓球（push stroke）中遇到机会球时进行扣杀，常带有突然性，往往可以直接得分。搓攻战术是乒乓球各种打法中都不可或缺的辅助战术。

## （二）方法（Methods）

（1）正、反手搓球结合（forehand and backhand push stroke）正手快拉（quick forehand topspin stroke）、快点、突击或扣杀。

（2）正、反手搓球结合反手快拉、快点、突击或扣杀。

## （三）注意事项（Precautions）

（1）搓攻战术既要尽可能早起板，以争取主动，又不能有急躁情绪，否则容易造成起板失误。

（2）在搓球中遇到机会球时要大胆扣杀，这是搓攻战术的主要得分手段。

（3）在搓短（short push）中摆短（drop shot），可使对方不易抢先进攻，有利于创造进攻机会，以便伺机用正、反手或侧身进攻（sideway attack）。

# 四、削中反攻战术（Chop and counter attack tactics）

## （一）特点（Characteristics）

由削球（chop）和攻球（attack）结合而成，常以逼角加转削球为主，伺机反攻，或以转、低、稳、变的削球，迫使对手在走动中拉攻，从而寻找机会，予以反攻。这种战术有"逼、变、凶、攻"（force, change, power, attack）的特点，是攻、削结合打法的主要战术。

## （二）方法（Methods）

（1）正、反手削球逼角，结合正手或侧身攻对方右侧空当。

（2）正、反手削两大角长球（deep ball），结合正、反手反攻。

## （三）注意事项（Precautions）

（1）正、反手削球都要注意旋转强度的变化。在削加转后用与其类似的手法削不转球，使对方拉出高球（lob），以进行反攻。

（2）削球时要尽可能压低弧线（trajectory），以避免对方扣杀或突击。

（3）削球逼角时要适当配以削另一角（the other corner），迫使对方在走动中击球。

# 五、发球抢攻战术(Attack after service tactics)

## (一)特点(Characteristics)

以旋转(spin)、线路(line)、落点(placement)以及速度(speed)不同的发球来增加对方回击的难度,使其出现机会球,或降低回球质量,然后抢先进攻,以争取主动或直接得分。这是乒乓球所有打法特别是进攻型打法的主要战术和得分手段。

## (二)方法(Methods)

(1)发下旋转与"不转"抢攻(attack in advance)。
(2)发正、反手奔球(topspin serve)抢攻。
(3)发正、反手侧上、下旋球抢攻。

## (三)注意事项(Precautions)

(1)发球要有线路和落点变化,以迫使对方在前、后、左、右走动中接发球。
(2)发球后要有抢攻准备,以保不失抢攻的机会。
(3)发球前要做好心理准备,对方可能以什么技术回击,这样才能做好抢攻准备。

# 六、接发球抢攻战术(Receive attack tactics)

## (一)特点(Characteristics)

以某一攻球技术形成的,进攻性强,可使接发球的不利地位变为主动地位,也可直接得分,是乒乓球运动中各种打法特别是进攻型打法的主要战术。

## (二)方法(Methods)

用快点、快攻或中等力量突击(make a sudden and violent drive)进行接发球抢攻。

## （三）注意事项（Precautions）

（1）由于接发球抢攻是在处于被动的接发球状态时所采取的进攻性打法，所以难度较大。接发球抢攻一般不可过凶，要看准来球的旋转方向（direction of rotation）、旋转强度（spin intensity）和高度（height），采用适当的方法进攻。例如对方发加转下旋球，接发球抢攻时则要采用提拉手法，以免下网。同时，攻球（attack）的力量不可过大。

（2）接发球抢攻动作结束后，要立即做好对攻或连续进攻的准备，以便继续处于主动地位。

（3）接发球抢攻、抢冲的力量越小，越应注意球的线路和落点，一般应多打在对方反手位置；若对方反手强而正手弱，则可多打在对方正手位置。

# 第五章　乒乓球技术教学
## （Table tennis teaching）

## 一、步法教学（Footwork teaching）

### （一）动作示范（Action demonstration）

教师示范（完整示范、分解示范）；挂图示范；视频示范（观看优秀运动员步法使用录像）。

### （二）动作讲解（Explanation for movement）

详细讲解步法的动作结构要领。动作重点在于：保持身体低重心（low gravity），脚尽量贴住地面移动（feet touch the floor）。其难点在于：步法的灵活运用（flexibility of footwork）。

### （三）练习步骤（Practice steps）

（1）单个步法（one step）或组合步法的徒手模仿练习。挥拍做单个步法，挥拍做碎步（quick short step），结合侧身步（sideway step）、侧身步结合交叉步（cross step）和并步（side step）练习，等等。

（2）看教师手势，练习者快速前、后、左、右变换移动，要求重心保持在同一水平面上。

（3）采用多球训练法（using the multi-ball training）。一组球的单个步法或多种步法组合练习可逐渐加大供球速度和难度。

（4）规定步法的次数或组数练习；或规定时间的步法练习。

（5）根据中国乒协制定的青少年《乒乓球教学训练大纲》规定的考核内容进行练习和测试。提高专项灵敏性、步法移动速度以及速度耐力。例如："8"字踩点、绕球台正面跑、移动换球、30 m×8 次往返跑，等等。

（6）移动换多球，在相距 3 m 的两条平行线之间进行。平行线外两端各放一筐球，球筐架高度是各年龄组使用球台的高度，球筐要求扁平，高度不超过

5 cm，直径不得超过20 cm。开始前，运动员站于左侧球筐，筐内装 15 只乒乓球，听到命令后右手至筐内拾一球，并迅速用滑步向右移动，其中球换左手，放入右侧球筐。再往返，直至左侧球筐 15 只球全部放入右侧球筐为止，计其所需时间。如果球脱手落地，裁判员立即补球放于左侧球筐。

（7）跳绳（skip），包括单摇跳和双摇跳两种。运动员双手持绳做好准备，听到命令后开始起跳，同时开表计时。双手摇绳一周、两脚分别着地一次为单摇跳绳一次。双手摇绳两周为双摇跳绳一次。记时 45 s 单摇或双摇跳绳的次数。运动员最多跳两次，两次之间的间歇时间 2 min，取其中最多的一次计算成绩。

（8）步法与手法综合练习。分别做小碎步（quick short step）、跳步（hop step）、并步（side step）、跨步（striding step）、交叉步（cross step）、侧身步（sideway step）的徒手推、搓、攻的动作练习。如推挡（block）（或快拨）中正手跨步攻球、推挡中侧身攻后扑正手、反手搓中侧身拉、左推右攻（并步移动）小碎步移动后跨步攻台内球、小碎步向后移动正手中远台攻球等等。

## （四）易犯错误与纠正方法（Misstep and correction）

（1）单步（one step）移动时，蹬地脚前脚掌无蹬旋动作，身体不稳定。

【纠正方法】　要求用前脚掌内侧蹬地并随着击球动作转动，保持身体的重心随挥拍动作向前移。

（2）并步（side step）移动时，来球方向的异侧脚蹬地后未及时向另一脚先并一小步。

【纠正方法】　提醒初学者牢记向右并步（right side step）时左脚先动、向左并步时右脚先动的顺序。

（3）跨步（striding step）时，蹬地一脚用力不够，蹬跨步幅（stride）小，速度慢。

【纠正方法】　一是腿部力量小，致使蹬踏无力，应加强腿部力量素质训练。二是不会用力，应强调运用前脚掌内侧蹬地。三是缺乏用力蹬地的意识，应加强用力蹬地与重心交换、位置移动、腰髋和上肢协调配合的意识训练。

（4）侧身步（sideway step）时，让不开身。

【纠正方法】　蹬地脚的前脚掌应在蹬地的同时要立即转动，才能转体让位。

（5）交叉步（cross step）时，过早伸手而没转腰击球，无法发力和迅速还原（recovery）。

【纠正方法】　练习者自我暗示"转腰击球"（contact），"先动脚后出手"。

(6)交叉步时,扑正手攻易向右后方跑动,延误回击时机。

【纠正方法】 要求练习者在上升期或高点期击球;或者专练正手位大角度短球;强化向右前方跑动的意识。

(7)两腿直立,肌肉僵硬,重心过高;或两脚分开过大,重心太低,无法用力蹬地。

【纠正方法】 要求练习者放松股四头肌、小腿三头肌等肌群,两脚间距略宽于肩,做原地的踝、膝屈伸运动,体会向前向上的蹬踏用力方法。强调脚对地面的蹬踏力是步法移动(footwork moving)的基础。

# 二、发球教学(Serve teaching)

## (一)动作示范(Action demonstration)

教师示范(完整示范、分解示范);视频示范(观看优秀运动员发球录像)。

## (二)动作讲解(Explanation for movement)

详细讲解发球的动作结构要领。动作重点在于:抛球、击球部位、用力方向。其难点在于:击球时机的把握和手腕发力的技巧。

## (三)练习步骤(Practice steps)

(1)采用平击发球(flat serve)方法进行讲解与示范。强调合法发球的重要性,熟悉发球的规则。

(2)徒手做抛球(throw)、引拍(backswing)与挥拍击球(contact)模仿练习。掌握发球时拍与球的时间、空间变化,保持合适的击球点。

(3)主练方做平击发球,陪练方用平挡球回接练习。主练者站在球台中间偏左位置,作中路直线的平击发球,一发一接,多次重复;先发直线(down the line)后发斜线(crosscourt),掌握挥拍路线和用力方向。

(4)主练方发各种急球练习。练习者发急球时,逐渐增大挥拍击球的速度和力量,掌握发球的用力大小和速度快慢变化。先练正手发急球后练反手发急球;先练习发斜线后练习发直线;速度(speed)由慢逐渐发力加快。同时,应强调抛球的高度(应高于16 cm)和下降期击球。练习者可先站在球台右半区,先练习正手发右方斜线长球,再练习右方直线长球。或站在左半台(left half court)侧身正手发左方斜线长球,再练习发左方直线长球。然后,根据此次序练习反手发急球。

（5）按规定发一种旋转球，对方采用平挡接发球的练习。练习者观察回接球的旋转方向变化，体会上旋（topspin）、下旋（backspin）、侧上旋（side topspin）、侧下旋（side backspin）等各种旋转球的反弹方向，掌握发各种旋转球的动作区别。

（6）采用同一动作手法发不同旋转和不同落点的球。提高发球技巧和变化，进一步体会拍触球的用力方向和方法。

（7）采用两种旋转结合发球至对方固定区域的练习。采用交替发侧上、下旋球或转与不转球。掌握用同种手法发不同旋转的方法和落点的准确性，体会摩擦球的击球部位（places of contact on the ball）、拍形角度（racket angle）、拍面方向（racket direction）和发力方向等。

（8）由低抛球逐渐增高抛球高度的高抛发球练习。掌握击球时机和全身的协调配合。

（9）结合比赛实践的练习。采用交替发左（右）侧上或下旋球或转与不转球（non‑spin ball），结合发球抢攻，教师可进行临场技术统计，有利于提高发球质量和在实战中的运用能力。

## （四）易犯错误与纠正方法（Misstep and correction）

（1）抛球（throwing）时，球未置于掌心。

【纠正方法】　讲解合法发球规则条文及其含义。明确合法抛球的概念，要求球不能触及手指及指根。

（2）抛球过低或不做抛球动作。

【纠正方法】　教师做正确的抛球示范动作，要求练习者作向上抛球的分解动作练习若干次，体会向上近乎垂直抛球时前臂和手腕（wrist）及手指动作。

（3）球（ball）和球拍（racket）相距太近，无法用力击球。

【纠正方法】　做抛球和向右后上方的挥臂引拍（backswing）模仿动作，明确加大拍与球的距离，便于加大击球瞬间的挥拍加速度。

（4）拍击球不准或击球点（contact point）过高、过低。

【纠正方法】　做徒手模仿练习。要求迎球挥拍（swing），首先肩关节部位尽量放松，使上臂迅速做出内收（adduction）与外展（extent）、前屈（forward bend）与后伸（rear protraction）、旋内（medial rotation）与旋外（lateral rotation）运动，保持球拍触及球时有合适的击球点。

（5）发出的球速度慢或旋转弱。

【纠正方法】　避免发力方法不正确缺乏爆发力（explosive power）。应放松执拍手各关节的肌肉，控制其作短促快速有力的收缩与放松，使作用力集中于球上。可徒手投掷乒乓球、羽毛球或石子，体会快速出手与顺势前送、迅速还原动作(recovery)。

(6)向前用力过多，或球下网。

【纠正方法】 应多向前下方发力。拍形可稍向前倾(上旋和侧上旋球)或稍后仰(急下旋和侧下旋球)，随时调节拍形角度变化。要求第一着台点不能离网太近，可在台面(play surface)上画出第一着台点的范围。

(7)向下用力过多、球反弹过高或出界。

【纠正方法】 此时应多向前用力。注意调节挥拍的路线(line)和方向(direction)。可做徒手模仿练习和教师示范动作，并可在台面上划出第一着台点的范围(range)，观摩优秀运动员发球技术录像。

# 三、接发球教学(Receiving teaching)

## (一)动作示范(Action demonstration)

教师示范(完整示范、分解示范)，视频示范(观看优秀运动员接发球录像)。

## (二)动作讲解(Explanation for movement)

详细讲解接发球的动作结构要领。动作重点在于：根据击球时球拍触球的位置、用力方向等，预判来球性质。其难点在于：灵活运用合理方法回击来球。

## (三)教学方法(Teaching methods)

(1)接发球与接发球抢攻应与发球练习紧密结合，相互促进。

(2)提高对球的旋转性能认识和理解，加强练习者对来球的反应与判断能力。

(3)提高练习者接发球的各种基本技术水平。技术水平愈高，接发球能力愈强。

(4)练习的难度应由易到难、由浅入深、循序渐进。从固定旋转、速度、落点的发球至复杂的综合性多种发球和接发球练习。

(5)加强手腕手指灵活性训练，以利调节拍形角度(racket angle)、拍面方向，尤其直握拍选手(pen-hold grip player)侧身接追身球，必须具备较好的手指手腕调控能力。庄则栋指出："加转发球、发球后抢攻、搓中突击(sudden drive while pushing strokes)、台内弹击(flick over table)等高难技巧，离开手腕的技能，犹如无米之炊。此外，击球角度（contact angle）的变化、节奏的变化、旋转的变化，这些都和手腕高技巧的功能分不开。"手指灵敏度高，对球可起"精调"作用。

（6）观看优秀运动员接发球技术录像。

### （四）练习步骤（Practice steps）

（1）回接对方平击发球（flat serve）练习。掌握接一般上旋球的方法。

（2）用推挡、快拨和快攻（fast attack）回接对方急球或侧上旋球练习。先接定点球，后接不定点球；先不固定回接球的落点（placement），后固定回接球的落点。

（3）用搓球或拉球回接对方发过来的加转（下旋）球练习。

（4）回接对方单一侧上或侧下（左或右）旋、固定发球落点的练习。

（5）用削球（chop）回接对方发长球（离端线30 cm区域）的练习。

（6）用快点回接对方发短球（short service）（离球网40 cm区域）的练习。

（7）回接对方两种旋转性能球，回击到对方台面固定区域练习。发球方任意发侧上、下旋或转与不转球，提高接发球方判断能力，各种接发球技巧及接发球准确性。

（8）接发球抢攻练习。

（9）提高第二板接发球、第四板接发球的衔接与进攻能力，提高接发球实战能力。对方连续发5~10个球或发一局球，本方连续接发球，计算得分与失分率。

（10）多球练习。对方用多球练习发球，限制其发球方法和旋转、速度、落点，另一方连续练接发球。

## 四、推挡教学（Block teaching）

### （一）动作示范（Action demonstration）

教师示范（完整示范、分解示范），视频示范（观看优秀运动员推挡技术录像）。

### （二）动作讲解（Explanation for movement）

详细讲解推挡的动作结构要领。动作重点在于：推挡球的时机和正确的用力方向。其难点在于：手腕灵活的控制、准确的线路落点。

### （三）练习步骤（Practice steps）

（1）徒手模仿练习。体会身体重心保持在两脚之间向前上方移动和前臂平行台面的挥动方法。

（2）平挡一板球练习。平挡对方发来的平击发球。可站在球台中间位置，沿中路直线方向平挡。体会手指、手腕的用力动作，调节拍形角度、拍面方向。

（3）对挡球练习。体会和掌握借力击球的方法和双手击球的节奏以及全身的协调配合。

（4）对推球练习。可进行左方斜线、右方斜线、左方直线、右方直线等基本击球路线练习。强调重心迎前击球（hit），手指和手腕应使拍面沿球体作弧形运动，亦称"包球"动作。

（5）划定落点的记板数练习。规定将球推挡到固定范围，并记每一个球连续对推的板数。提高推挡（block）的准确性、掌握双方击球的节奏。逐渐要求加快击球速度和力量，记录在规定时间内（如30 s、60 s）累计推挡球的板数。

（6）一快推一加力推练习。体会击球时的借力与发力方法，掌握击球点、发力方向与发力方法。

（7）推挡对方快攻球或扣杀球（smash）练习。体会推挡时加力与减力方法，以及击球落点的变化。

（8）推挡对方弧圈球练习。体会推强烈上旋球的引拍位置、击球时机、发力方向和方法。提高推挡弧圈球能力。

（9）采用推挤与加力推（punch block）结合回击弧圈球练习。进一步掌握对付弧圈球的能力，提高准确性和实战性。

（10）加强步法与手法的协调配合，采用两点推回对方一点练习。陪练者可将球推或攻至对方左、右两点，主练者在移动中用推挡将球回击到对方一点。体会在移动中保持合适的击球点和拍面方向。

（11）一点推两点或推三点练习。提高推挡时的落点变化能力。体会击球的拍面方向、拍形角度和推挡变线的发力方向，以及手臂、手指与手腕调节球拍的动作。

（12）推下旋球练习。两人快推中一人作推下旋球或对方发侧下旋长球（deep side backspin serve），主练者做推下旋球练习，体会触球时的切球（slice）动作。拇指稍用力，手腕稍用力向外转动。

（13）在接发球中推对方直线或斜线（crosscourt）练习。提高在前4板球中推挡使用率和准确性。

（14）教学比赛。规定发上旋球（topspin）或侧上旋球，形成以推攻为主的比赛，提高各种推挡技术的运用水平。

## （四）易犯错误与纠正方法（Misstep and correction）

（1）握拍方法不准确。食指勾拍柄（handle of racket）或拇指过分用力，拍形后仰（racket tilted backward）。击球中下部（blow center），弧线（trajectory）过高。

【纠正方法】 讲解与示范正确的握拍方法和动作要点，建立正确的动作概念。要求拇指和食指间应有一指宽的距离，相对握于拍肩部位两侧，便于交替用力。

（2）站位时右脚在前、前后开立，不易照顾正手位来球。

【纠正方法】 讲解准备姿势动作要点，让其接一正手位来球，体会不正确站位（stance）的欠缺。做若干次两脚平行站立或左脚稍前的推挡徒手模仿练习，建立正确的动力定型（dynamic stereotypy）。

（3）推挡时拍面前倾不够，击球出界。

【纠正方法】 要求练习者放松执拍手（racket hand）的各关节，大臂和肘关节靠近身体，使前臂做旋外、手腕作外展和屈的动作；同时放松拇指，食指稍用力压拍，增加拍面前倾角度。

（4）挡球（block）时，拍身下垂，形成"吊拍"，击球易下网。

【纠正方法】 要求大臂（upper arm）和肘关节靠近身体，前臂作旋外，使拍身和拍柄呈半横状，便于推压球。

（5）推挡时拍面过于前倾，击球出界（contact off the table）。

【纠正方法】 因手腕过于固定，拇指第一关节僵直，使拍形角度无法调节变化。练习者一手持拍，一手持球，使拍面在球体上作摩擦滚动动作，体会手指手腕调节拍形角度用力方法。

（6）推挡时击球时机晚，形成托球弧线过高或击球下网。

【纠正方法】 应提高反应判断能力；加强击球后顺势前送（follow-through）、迅速还原的执拍手协调性徒手挥拍练习（practice of swing）。此外，明确各种推挡球的击球时机概念。

（7）推挡时未迎前击球，摩擦动作差，球出界或下网。

【纠正方法】 应使两脚前脚掌内侧蹬地用力使身体重心前倾，才可保证击球的稳定性。采用摩擦"带轴"球练习，体会手指手腕持拍边碰撞球边沿球体摩擦的"微调"动作（推挡球以碰撞为主）。此外，可观看优秀运动员的推挡球技术录像。

# 五、攻球教学(Attack teaching)

## (一)动作示范(Action demonstration)

教师示范(完整示范、分解示范);挂图示范;视频示范(观看优秀运动员攻球录像)。

## (二)动作讲解(Explanation for movement)

详细讲解攻球的动作结构要领。动作重点在于:击球的部位以及发力透过球心。其难点在于:击球时机(contact timing)的把握。

## (三)练习步骤(Practice steps)

(1)徒手模仿练习(imitation without racket)。首先建立各种攻球技术的正确动作概念。掌握击球时引拍位置、挥拍路线(path of the racket)、拍面方向、拍形角度(racket angle)、身体各部位的协调配合等各种攻球步法。

(2)攻一板球练习。攻对方发出的一般上旋球(topspin)。如对方平击发球(flat service),主练者正(反)手攻一板球,再重新发球。随着技术水平的提高,逐渐增加发球的旋转、力量、速度和落点变化,练习各种攻球动作。掌握击球时机、击球部位(places of contact)和用力方法,确保有合适的击球点(contact point)。

(3)攻平挡球练习。对方采用平挡供球,主练者正(反)手攻球。体会借力击球的轻打用力方法,掌握挥拍路线及拍触球动作及全身协调配合。如一挡一攻右方斜线或中路直线。

(4)正手对攻练习。双方均采用正手攻球,如右方斜线对攻,左方斜线侧身正手对攻、中路或左、右三条直线对攻。掌握攻球的节奏变化和重心转换、发力方向与发力方法。

(5)左推右攻的定点练习。陪练者反手快推左方斜线和左方直线至对方左、右两点,主练者采用反手快推左方斜线、正手快攻右方直线至对方左半台的两点打一点。掌握手法与步法(footwork)结合,提高推、攻结合及左、右摆速。

(6)正(反)手两点攻一点的定点练习。陪练者反手推挡将球推到攻球者台面左、右两点,主练者在移动中将球攻回一点。提高攻球者判断与移动能力,进一步掌握击球时的拍形角度、拍面方向、击球时机、发力方向。

（7）正手三点（或多点）攻一点练习。陪练者反手推挡将球推到攻球者台面左、中、右三点（或多点），主练者在移动中将球攻回对方一点。由定点的有规律练习，逐渐增加难度至不定点的无规律练习。进一步提高攻球的稳定性（consistence）和准确性。

（8）正（反）手一点攻两点练习。主练者用正（反）手攻球将球攻至对方左、右两点，陪练者用推挡或左推右攻（backhand block with forehand attack）将球击回一点。提高攻球变线能力。

（9）推挡侧身攻扑正手练习。陪练者推左方斜线，在对推中主练者侧身攻中，陪练者伺机推直线至主练者正手位，主练者采用交叉步（cross step）扑正手攻。提高左半台进攻能力和全台跑动攻的步法移动速度和攻球准确性。

（10）正手中远台对攻练习。双方站在离台70 cm以外区域进行攻球，主练者可逐渐向远台移位攻球。掌握中远台攻球的击球时机、击球部位、拍形角度、发力方向和发力方法，以及前后移动的步法。

## （四）易犯错误与纠正方法（Misstep and correction）

（1）直握拍者（pen-hold grip player）引拍未到身体右侧方，挥拍时前臂向左前方过多，球易从对方边线飞出界外。

【纠正方法】 做徒手模仿练习。要求两脚开立，左脚稍前站立。引拍的位置和高度在体侧和髋关节处，拍面方向正对来球方向。大臂带动前臂向前向左上方挥拍。

（2）拍面前倾过多，攻球下网。

【纠正方法】 避免手腕僵硬、拇指用力压拍过大；或攻球时摩擦球过多而向前打的力量小。做攻一板球练习，体会正确的用力方法和发力方向。

（3）挥拍攻球时，抬肘过高击球弧线低或球下网。

【纠正方法】 因大臂外展过多使肘关节偏高，练习者应使肩关节（shoulder）肌肉群放松，防止提肩；保持上臂和身体的夹角约30°左右。一般用非执拍手（free hand）握拳横置身体右腋下，自测大臂和身体之间距离。防止大臂外展角度过大。

（4）快攻时，击球点（hit of point）在身体右侧后方，下降期击球。

【纠正方法】 因挥拍时大臂后摆过多，称为"拉后手"；且还原慢，无法在身前和上升期击球，可观看优秀运动员攻球技术录像，建立正确的快攻动作概念；背靠墙站立，做徒手模仿练习，要求球拍和手臂不能碰墙，防止向后挥拍时动作过大，掌握合适的击球点。

（5）反手攻时，未运用爆发力而是借力推击球。

【纠正方法】 做好击球前的引拍动作(backswing)，使拍与球保持一定的距离以便加大挥拍的力量，主动发力攻球。做攻一板球练习，逐渐加大攻球力量。

(6)拉攻时，向前用力过多，拉球下网。

【纠正方法】 拉球的发力方向应向上前方，即向上力量大于向前的力量。拍触球时，打摩结合以摩为主。明确动作的概念，观看技术录像，用多球练习拉一板球。掌握正确的发力方向和发力方法。

(7)快点时，重心(center of gravity)未跟上，攻球(attack)弧线低，易下网。

【纠正方法】 首先解决步法移动的重心转换；解决上步后怕回不来的思想。要求击球到位，充分发挥前臂和手腕的快速挥动动作，采用多球练习方法，发近网短球，主练者根据来球的旋转性能，迅速上步快点，并立即移步还原。

(8)杀高球时，引拍动作小，压不住球或击球无力。

【纠正方法】 因来球弧线高，打出距离较长，应多向后向上引拍，保持足够的拍与球的距离，加大挥拍的路线和杀球力量。徒手模仿练习后，杀对方放过来的一板球，要求练习者做出"弧形"挥拍动作。

# 六、搓球教学(Push teaching)

## (一)动作示范(Action demonstration)

教师示范(完整示范、分解示范)；挂图教学；视频示范(观看优秀运动员搓球录像)。

## (二)动作讲解(Explanation for movement)

详细讲解搓球的动作结构要领。动作重点在于：击球时往前下方发力，以及击球的中下部。其难点在于：判断来球旋转强度与自己拍面的角度控制。

## (三)练习步骤(Practice steps)

(1)徒手模仿搓球动作练习。徒手模仿或徒手搓带轴球，建立各种搓球动作的正确概念和摩擦球方法。

(2)自抛自搓一板球练习。自己抛球(throwing)至本方台面，根据不同的击球时机、击球部位和拍面角度变化将球搓(chop)过去。掌握搓球的用力方向和方法。

（3）搓对方下旋发球（backspin service）的一板球练习。陪练者可正手或反手发下旋球，主练者练习用搓球接发球。发球的落点可由定点至不定点，旋转强度和变化可逐渐增大。提高搓球的协调性和稳定性。

（4）对搓练习。先固定练习路线（line），例如双方用反（正）手对搓中路直线、左方斜线、左方直线、右方斜线、右方直线，提高搓球的准确性。先练慢搓后练快搓与转与不转球，提高搓球的节奏和旋转变化。

（5）两点搓回对方一点练习。陪练者将球先搓至主练者球台的左、右两点，主练者采用正、反手搓球将球回至对方一点。由定点的有规律练习至不定点的无规律练习。加强正、反手搓球（backhand push）的落点与旋转变化和摆动速度。

（6）一点搓不同落点练习。陪练者将球搓至主练者台面某固定一点，主练者根据练习要求，采用不同搓球动作将球搓至对方任何一点，对方可用多球供球，提高搓球的落点变化能力。

（7）左搓右拉、搓中侧身正手拉、反手搓反手拉、搓中侧身正手拉扑正手攻等搓与拉的结合练习，提高在实战中搓球运用能力。

（8）教学比赛。规定发球的方法：下旋球（backspin）或左（右）侧下旋球，以搓球回接，形成以搓攻为主的比赛。提高在实战中的搓球运用能力。

## （四）易犯错误与纠正方法（Misstep and correction）

（1）引拍时，拍面过于后仰，出高球或球不过网。

【纠正方法】 做徒手模仿练习，要求前臂做旋外（supination）、手腕做伸、放松拇指，食指和中指稍用力保持拍形稍后仰（racket tilted slightly backward），有利于加大来球的反作用力。

（2）引拍高度不够，回球下旋力不强。

【纠正方法】 做自抛自搓（push）一板球练习。要求上臂前屈角度加大，前臂持球拍上引，利于加大由上向下切球的动作。

（3）手臂和手指、手腕肌肉未协调放松，不易加速挥拍主动发力摩擦球。回球不转或下网。

【纠正方法】 做持拍或不持拍的徒手模仿练习。体会执拍手各关节的肌肉收缩与放松协调配合，提高击球的感觉能力。也可结合做自抛自搓的一板球练习，体会肌肉快速攻缩的发力方法。

（4）拍触球一瞬间，前臂和手腕未做旋内与前屈外展，未向前摩擦前送，回球下网或不转。

【纠正方法】　做徒手或摩擦"带轴"球练习。体会拍触球时向前下方的边摩擦边前送动作,掌握前臂、手指手腕调节拍面角度、击球部位、交替用力方法。

(5)击球时,拍面后仰角度小,回球下网或不转,打出高球(lob)。

【纠正方法】　搓接对方发来的下旋球练习。体会拍面角度(racket angle)的变化,掌握前臂、手指手腕使拍面后仰在下降期击球中下部和前送的动作。

(6)拍触球时,手臂前送动作过大,肘关节僵直,还原动作慢。回球出界或下网。

【纠正方法】　做徒手模仿练习。体会击球时快速运用爆发力(explosive power)和顺势前送、迅速还原动作。也可做单线对搓练习,提高击球的协调性和节奏感。

(7)击球时,球接触球拍的部位不准,回球不转,出界或下网。

【纠正方法】　建立正确的各种搓球动作概念,明确搓加转与不转球的球触拍部位。加强对来球落点(placement)和飞行弧线的判断以及执拍手各关节在引拍时的调节作用,使球拍挥动时拍面方向对准来球。做搓接对方发球的一板球练习(采用单球或多球练习方法)。提高判断反应能力与协调性。

(8)摩擦球无力,回球下网。

【纠正方法】　做徒手模仿或搓接一板球练习。要求从两脚前脚掌内侧蹬地用力,将力迅速从下肢、躯干、执拍手臂(racket arm)传递到手腕(wrist)和手指(finger)上。掌握运用全身协调用力方法,防止仅上肢发力而下肢不动的缺点。

# 七、拉球教学(Topspin stroke teaching)

## (一)动作示范(Action demonstration)

教师示范(完整示范、分解示范);挂图示范;视频示范(观看优秀运动员拉球录像)。

## (二)动作讲解(Explanation for movement)

详细讲解拉球的动作结构要领。动作重点在于:击球部位(striking spot on the ball),摩擦球面,力量方向。其难点在于:击球时机的把握,身体的协调用力。

## （三）练习步骤（Practice steps）

（1）徒手挥拍练习。一是学习完整的拉弧圈球技术动作。二是在全身协调用力基础上，体会前臂及手腕（wrist）的发力动作。

（2）自抛自拉练习。一是学习拉弧圈球的完整动作。二是学习和体会球拍以何种角度对球进行摩擦（friction）。初步建立手上的感觉。

（3）一人发正手位斜线平击球（flat stroke），另一人练习拉弧圈球（loop）。一是学会在什么击球时机（hitting time）拉球。二是将自抛自拉摩擦球的感觉转移到此项练习中来。

（4）一人发正手位斜线下旋球，另一人练习拉弧圈球。一是学会拍面的调节。二是学会拉球时动作的有效用力，即在全身协调用力的基础上，前臂加速收缩和手腕用力。

（5）多球练习。一是通过多球进行大量的重复性练习（repetitive practice），以利于动作概念的建立及拉球能力的提高。二是送不同落点（placement）的球，学会用步法找好拉球的合理位置。三是送不同旋转的球，学会比较自如地调整好拍面角度、发力方向和控制好力量。

（6）一推一拉练习、一搓一拉练习、一削一拉练习。单线练习的重点是学会在一个固定区域内找准来球位置，完成拉球技术动作。有规律（regularly）复线练习的重点是学会在两个固定区域内，有规律地运用步法移动（footwork movement）来找准回击球的位置，在移动中完成拉球技术动作。无规律复线练习的重点是学会在两个固定区域内，根据无规律地（irregularly）运用步法及时抢位（take position），在判断和移动中完成拉球技术动作。

## （四）易犯错误与纠正方法（Misstep and correction）

（1）站位或远或近，找不准击球点（hitting point）。

【纠正方法】　在固定点上反复做拉球练习，建立击球点和站位关系的动作概念。

（2）引拍动作小或不及时，导致无法用力摩擦球。

【纠正方法】　徒手挥拍练习，注意加大引拍动作并保持适度放松。

（3）拍面过分前倾（forward）或后仰（backward），导致击不准球、下网，或在击球时击打多摩擦少。

【纠正方法】　固定好正确的拍面角度，拉自抛球。体会拍面角度（racket angle）和击球部位的关系。

（4）挥拍（swing）过于向前或向上方。过于向前方导致球没有一个适当的弧线，容易下网；过于向上方导致球有一个较大的弧线，由于缺乏向前的力量，使球下网。

【纠正方法】 如果挥拍过于向前方，可用拉下旋球的方法来纠正。让练习者多注意摩擦(friction)球的中部。如果是挥拍动作过于向上，可以用拉上旋球(topspin stroke)的方法来纠正，让练习者多注意摩擦球的中上部。

（5）拍触球时发不出力或摩擦不住球，致使球没有充分的旋转和弧线。

【纠正方法】 摩擦球时要求练习者发力要集中，并注意在迎球挥拍过程中，手臂保持适当的放松，以利于前臂的瞬间发力。可以让练习者自抛自拉的办法，来体会球拍触球时如何用力和摩擦住球，同时注意两腿的重心转换、转髋、转肩带臂(shoulder leads arm recovery)和前臂及手腕在触球瞬间的协同发力动作。

（6）拉球动作僵硬或触球后突然停顿，影响拉球动作的连贯性(continuity)和技术质量。

【纠正方法】 在肌肉放松的前提下，做拉弧圈球的徒手练习，要求动作做完整。用多球进行上述要求的拉球练习。

# 八、乒乓球双打技术教学(Doubles teaching)

## (一)双打特点(Doubles characteristic)

双打是两人协同作战，因此，要求两人在思想上必须取得一致，相互信任、相互鼓励、相互谅解；要求具有灵活的步法(footwork)和在走动中间击各种不同来球的能力；要求在技术、战术上能够默契配合，协调一致，共同创造战机，充分发挥两人的技术水平。

## (二)双打配对与位置移动(Doubles match and location moving)

### 1. 双打配对(doubles match)

（1）两人具有较好的协同作战的思想基础。

（2）在站位(stance)和走位(block)的方式上，两人最好具有不同的特点，以利于灵活地交换击球位置(hitting place)。

（3）技术上各种比较有利的配对是：

①一人左手握拍，一人右手握拍。

②一人为近台快攻，一人为中台攻击(最好还能拉弧圈球)。

③两个削、攻结合型（attacking chop）。

**2. 双打位置移动（location moving）**

（1）对双打位置移动的要求：
①不影响同伴（partner）的视线和判断来球；
②不妨碍同伴抢占击球位置和回击来球；
③有利于本身回击下次来球。
（2）各种配对常用的位置移动方法：
①左手握拍和右手握拍（grip）配对时，常用横斜向或横向的移动方法。一般在打完球后，向自己的反手一侧移动。
②两个右手握拍配对时，常用三角形的移动方法。
③左推右攻（backhand block with forehand attack）和两面攻配对时，左推右攻者多作左右移动，两面攻者多作前后移动。
④近台攻击（close-to-table play）和中台攻击配对时，近台攻击者多作横向移动，中台攻击者多作横斜向的移动。
⑤两个削、攻结合配对时，一般用横斜方向的移动方法，或作环形移动。如果是近削和远削配对，则近削者（chopper）以横斜向移动为主，远削者以前后移动为主。

## （三）双打发球与接发球（Doubles serve and receive）

**1. 双打发球（doubles serve）**

发球必须控制对方的进攻（attack），常以发"短、低、转"（short，low，spin）球为主，即发球不出台、弧线低、旋转变化强，再配合其他发球，使对方难以抢攻，减少同伴防守困难。
（1）发球争取直接得分。应发各种不同旋转、速度和落点变化的球，使对方不易接发球抢攻或直接失分。同时，要果断地进行抢攻（attack in advance），并且又要做好积极防御球台（playing surface）两角的准备。一旦发现对手接发球控制比较好时，要及时改用中等力量进攻对方的弱点，先上手掌握主动权，为同伴创造下一板连续进攻的机会。
（2）发球要有利于同伴特长技术发挥。如果同伴擅长拉弧圈球（loop），应先发近网强下旋球（heavy backspin serve），迫使对方用搓回接，为同伴抢拉创造时机（timing）。
双打发球必须遵循"快、短、低"（quick，short，low）的原则，即发球出手速度快，有突然性，落点短，不出台或似出台非出台，弧线（arc）低。这样才能遏制对方的攻势，为自己的同伴创造抢攻条件。实践证明，大多数双打选手，一般均将球发至对方球台的中线近网处。

由于双打的接发球范围比单打（single's）缩小了一半，因而给接发球抢攻（或抢拉）提供比较有利的条件。为压抑对方的接发球抢攻（抢拉）和有利于本方的发球抢攻（attack after serve），常用的发球有：

①当对方接发球抢攻（attack in advance）（或抢拉）比较厉害时，发转与不转的近网短球至中线附近，能比较有效地压抑对方的攻势；如配合发急球（fast ball）和左侧上、下旋球至中线附近，还能获得进攻的机会。

②对方站位较近时，可发正手大角度的"奔球"或追身球（body hit）；对方准备用正手接发球时，可发急下旋或侧上、下旋（backspin）至中线附近；对方准备用反手接球时，则可发正手大角度球。这些发球均能加大对方接发球的难度，有利于同伴的回击。

③发右侧上、下旋球至中线（center line）附近，配合发急球，创造进攻机会。

④根据对方接发球的弱点和本方同伴抢攻的需要来确定发球的方式和落点。

**2. 双打接发球（doubles receive）**

双打的接发球技术与单打基本相同，但因多接的是不出台的球，故必须首先练好接各种短球（drop shot）的技术，越全面越好。采用点（flick）、拉（loop）、拨、推（block）、攻（attack）、冲（rush）、撇侧旋（make sidespin）、搓（push）、拧、弹、挑（flip）、摆短（drop shot）等。由于双打接发球的范围较小，来球落点较易判断，稍作移动即可抢占合理的击球位置，而且接发球的落点又不受发球区的限制，因此，应当充分利用这些有利条件，千方百计地在接发球时抢攻或抢拉，以争取主动。如果发球一方控制严密，确实难于做到接发球抢攻或抢拉时，应当注意：

①以短摆短（drop shot），不给对方发球抢攻或抢拉。

②回击对方的右大角，造成对方交换击球位置（hitting area）的困难。

③根据对方下次击球者的弱点，确定接发球的方式和落点，为同伴进攻创造机会。

**（四）乒乓球双打的练习方法（Doubles practice steps）**

（1）徒手模仿双打练习。根据不同类型打法的配对，做各种位置移动的步法练习，提高双打走位配置和移动速度(movement speed)。

（2）多球练习。主练者在走位中连续轮流做快攻(drive stroke)、拉攻(topspin stroke)或快拉(quick topspin stroke)等攻球练习，提高双打的走位配合和移动速度。

（3）一方发球和发球抢攻为主的练习。主练者发球，陪练者将球回接至固定区域，主练者抢攻。逐渐加大难度，陪练者将球回至不固定的区域(area)，主练者抢攻，提高双打前三板进攻能力。

（4）一方接发球(serve)或接发球抢攻为主的练习。陪练者发球，可限制球旋转或落点(placement)，主练者接发球或接发球抢攻。再逐渐加大难度，陪练者发不同旋转和落点球，主练者抢攻，提高双打前三板(first three strokes)进攻能力。

（5）及时调整基本站位的练习(事先颠倒基本站位，要求在练习开始后1~2个回合中，迅速将位置调整过来)。

（6）一人帮助两人双打(doubles)的练习。即单人对双人的练习。如一人用攻(attack)、推(block)、搓(push)等各种技术将球击至对方台面(playing surface)，主练者在走位中轮流将击球击回一点，提高相持中控制能力、击球准确性和步法移动速度。

（7）记分练习。可进行单个战术的计分比赛，或关键球的记分比赛，或一局、一场教学比赛(teaching skills competition)，提高双打的实战能力(competition ability)。

# 第六章　乒乓球技术课双语课堂教学
# （Table tennis skill lesson bilingual teaching）

本章介绍一些常用句型（common sentence patterns）。

## 一、考勤（Attendance）

| | |
|---|---|
| Is there anyone absent? | 有人缺席吗？ |
| Who is absent? | 谁没有出席？ |
| What's the matter with Zhao Ming? | 赵明怎么了？／赵明有什么事吗？ |
| What's wrong with him? | 他怎么了？／他出了什么问题？ |
| Do you know where Wu Xiaoli is? | 你知道吴小利在哪儿吗？ |
| I have no idea where he is. | 我不知道他在哪里。 |
| I'm afraid he can't come today. | 恐怕他今天不能来。 |
| He doesn't feel well. | 他觉得身体不大舒服。 |
| You are late again today. | 你今天又迟到了。 |
| Why are you often late for class? | 你为什么上课经常迟到？ |
| You have been five minutes late. | 你迟到了五分钟。 |
| Where have you been? | 你到哪里去了？ |
| Did you oversleep? | 你睡过头了吗？ |
| Don't be late again next time. | 下次不要迟到。 |
| Try to be here on time. | 要准时到这里。 |
| Enter the rank. We can start now. | 入列。我们可以开始了。 |
| Hurry up! It's time for class. | 快！上课的时间到了。 |
| It's time to start now. | 现在要开始（上课）了。 |
| Come here! We'll begin in no time. | 过来！我们马上就要开始了。 |
| There goes the bell. | （上课）铃响了。 |
| Silence, please. I'm going to call the roll. | 请安静，我要点名了。 |
| Are you ready to begin? | 你们准备好开始了吗？ |
| Let's get started! | 让我们开始吧！ |

# 二、介绍(Introduction)

| | |
|---|---|
| Allow me to introduce myself. | 请允许我自我介绍。 |
| My name is Zhang Gang. | 我的名字叫张刚。 |
| I come from Class 5. | 我来自5班。 |
| I'm your teacher for table tennis lesson. | 我是你们的乒乓球老师。 |
| Let me introduce Huang Huo, captain of your table tennis team. | 让我来介绍我们的乒乓球队长黄火。 |
| We've been looking forward to meeting the new teacher for table tennis lesson. | 我们一直盼望见到乒乓球课的新老师。 |

# 三、队形学习术语(Terms used for rank formation drills)

| | |
|---|---|
| Attention! | 立正! |
| Halt! | 立定! |
| At ease! | 稍息! |
| Call the roll! | 点名! |
| Eyes front! | 向前看! |
| Eyes right! | 向右看齐! |
| Fall in! | 集合! |
| Close ranks! | 向前靠拢! |
| Dismiss! | 解散! |
| Fall out! | 就地解散! |
| Hold your position! | 原地不动! |
| All present! | 全到! |
| Out of ranks! | 出列! |
| Into the rank! | 入列! |
| Line up! In two files (ranks). | 整队! 两路纵队(两列横队)! |
| Make fours(file/rank), fall in! | 站四列(路)纵(横)队! |
| Extend! Make room(Keep space). | 散开! 保持距离。 |
| Guide on Liu Jun! Guide Centre! | 以刘军为基准 向中(前)看齐! |
| Face about! | 向后转! |
| Forward march! | 齐步——走! |
| Double (time) march! | 跑步——走! |

| Left turn! Right turn! About turn! | 向左型！向右转！向后转！ |
| One step forward! Three steps backward! | 向前一步——走！退后三步——走！ |
| Right wheel! | 右转弯走！ |
| About face march! | 向后转走！ |
| Count/number off！ | 报数！ |
| By twos number！ | 一、二报数！ |
| Single rank split! Make twos, fall in! | 一列横队成两列横队——走！ |
| Two files split! Make fours, fall in! | 两路纵队成四路纵队——走！ |
| Keep space on both sides! | 保持两边的距离！ |
| Please stand at the end of the line! | 请站队尾！ |
| Boys and girls, please march in step. | 同学们，要步伐整齐。 |
| First of all. Let's do some formation drills. | 首先让我们做队形操练。 |
| Listen carefully to my commands. | 请注意我的口令。 |
| Please react and move as you can. | 要尽快反应和移动。 |
| Quick！Fall in at the end of the line. | 快！排到队伍的末尾去。 |

# 四、准备活动(Warming-up)

| Let's do the warming-up together. | 我们一起做准备活动。 |
| First, Let's do jogging. | 首先，我们慢跑。 |
| Arms forward( raise)！ | 两手前平举！ |
| Arms sideways! | 两手侧平举！ |
| Head stretch! | 头部运动！ |
| Neck stretch! | 颈部运动！ |
| Shoulder stretch! | 肩部运动！ |
| Waist stretch! | 腰部运动！ |
| Hip stretch! | 髋部运动！ |
| Knee stretch! | 膝部运动！ |
| Ankle stretch! | 踝部运动！ |
| Chest stretch! | 扩胸运动！ |
| Easy run! | 放松跑！ |
| Standing hamstring stretch! | 压腿！ |
| Hip flexor stretch! | 弓箭步压腿！ |
| Adductor stretch! | 仆步压腿！ |

# 五、引导（Guidance）

Today we are going to learn chop.　今天我们要学习削球技术。

First I'd like to introduce the new rules of table tennis to you, and then show you how to serve.　我会先向你们介绍乒乓球新规则，接着给你们讲解如何发球。

Today we are mainly learning returning serve.　今天我们主要学习接发球。

First, we shall spend half an hour in footwork. Next, you will continue with serving.　我们先用半小时练习步法，然后继续练发球。

What I shall explain is the basic ways of serving.　我要讲解的是发球的基本方法。

Today we'll study Lesson Four "Table Tennis Rules" and I am sure that you have previewed it.　今天我们将学习第四课"乒乓球规则"，我相信你们已经预习了这一课。

The main task of this lesson is to get command of the classification of table tennis tactics.　本课的主要任务是掌握乒乓球的战术分类。

The key points of the unit are the history of table tennis.　该单元的主要内容是乒乓球的历史。

It is well known that China is adominant nation in table tennis world. Many foreign players and coaches have come to China to learn experience.　众所周知，中国是国际乒坛上的领军之国。很多外国球员和教练员都来中国取经。

# 六、示范（Demonstration）

Counter-drive 30 times.　对攻 30 次。

Watch my serving, and then do the same.　看我发球，然后照做。

Please watch my forearm movements.　看我的前臂动作。

Who would like to be the first one to try?　谁愿意第一个来试一试？

Watch closely my demonstration of the　请仔细观看我的动作示范。

movement.

Before you serve, let me tell you how to do it.

发球前，让我告诉你们怎么做。

Let me explain the trick for serving.

我要说一说发球的技巧。

Let me explain the key point of push stroke.

我讲解下搓球的关键动作要领。

Ready position.

选位。

Feet shoulder-width apart or wider.

两脚开立略比肩宽。

Feet staggered, right foot slightly behind left

两脚稍分前后，左脚在前右脚在后。

Knees bent.

膝盖稍弯。

Weight on forefoot.

重心在前脚上。

Backswing.

引拍。

Bring racket back to center of body.

将球拍引至身体中部。

Racket in open position to allow it to contact bottom of ball.

球拍后仰，确保能击球底部。

Contact.

击球。

Forearm extends to bring racket to ball.

前臂向前伸展，带动球拍击向球。

Racket contacts ball when the ball begins to descend from top of bounce.

在来球的下降期，球拍触球。

Point of contacts with ball is fairly close to body.

击球时尽量使球离身体较近些。

Racket contacts ball below ball's center.

击球的中下部。

Wrist snaps forward at contact.

手腕抖动向前发力击球。

Follow-through.

（挥拍）跟随。

Racket continues toward intended target.

球拍继续向目标方向顺势前送。

Recovery.

还原。

After chop returns to ready position.

搓球顺势前送完成后，迅速还原成搓球前的准备姿势。

# 七、要求（Requesting）

Please do what I have told you.

请按我说的做。

First, turn around and face the class.

首先，转过身来面对全班。

Please do exercises for five minutes.

请做五分钟练习。

Go on doing push stroke for five minutes, please.

请继续做五分钟推球练习。

| | |
|---|---|
| Does anyone want to give us a demonstration? | 有人愿意给我们做个示范吗? |
| Who wants to repeat the action again? | 谁愿意把这个动作再重复一遍? |
| Would you like to try it? | 你愿意试一下吗? |
| Could you help me pick up the ball? | 你能帮我捡球吗? |
| Would you come to the front, Zhang Ming? | 张明到前边来, 好吗? |
| Can you tell me how to push stroke again? | 你能再讲一遍怎么推球吗? |
| Try to practice push stroke after class. | 课后尽可能练习推球。 |
| Would you mind relaxing more? | 请放松些可以吗? |
| Please respect others! | 请尊重他人! |
| Be quick! Be quiet! Be neat! | 快! 静! 齐! |
| Let's have a game! | 我们来做个游戏! |
| Who can help him? | 谁能帮他? |
| Don't disturb others! | 不要干扰他人! |
| Come out! Go back! | 出来! 回去! |
| Please stand behind! | 请站后面! |
| Your free hand cannot hide the ball. | 你的手不能遮挡球。 |
| Watch me first, and then copy me. | 先看着我做, 然后模仿。 |
| Watch me do this movement. | 看我做这个移动。 |
| Let's watch him do sidestep and point out his weak points. | 我们注意看他做并步, 并指出他的不足之处。 |
| Don't shake your body, do it like this. | 身子不要摇晃, 这样做。 |
| The right way to serve is like this. | 发球的正确方式是这样的。 |
| Come out to the front and show everybody else. | 到前面来, 做给大家看。 |
| Please do the movement by the numbers. Do combination exercises in twos /in pairs. | 按口令做这个动作。两人一组/成对做组合练习。 |
| Be divided into 2 groups, each group of 4 people. | 分成 2 个组, 每组 4 人。 |
| Be divided into 6 groups, each group of 4 people. | 分成 6 个组, 每组 4 人。 |
| Practice group to serve. | 分组练习发球。 |
| Do drills collectively /individually/in turn. | 集体(单人、轮流)做练习。 |
| We shall do the practice in the | 我们将按下列方法做练习。 |

following way.

| | |
|---|---|
| Practice serving in the same way as last time. | 用与上次一样的方法练发球。 |
| Take a step (half a step) forward. | 向前迈一步(半步)。 |
| We shall divide into two teams to play team games next time. | 下次我们将分成两队打团体赛。 |

## 八、劝告(Advice)

| | |
|---|---|
| It would be much perfect if you can keep your body more balanced. | 如果你能使身体平稳些,那就更好了。 |
| It would be better if you paid more attention to the push stroke. | 如果你多注意一下推球,就会更好了。 |
| It would be more correct to snap your forearm. | 收小臂就更正确了。 |
| It'll be a good idea for you to have more practice when you have time. | 在有时间时多做练习是个好主意。 |
| I think you ought to repeat block exercises several times. | 我认为你应该做几遍推挡练习。 |
| I think that you should go to review yesterday's movements. | 我觉得你应该去复习昨天的动作。 |
| You should play table tennis every day in order to improve it. | 你们应该天天打乒乓球以提高技术。 |
| Why don't you come here earlier? | 你为什么不早一点来? |
| Why not discuss this table tennis tactic? | 为什么不讨论这个乒乓球战术? |

## 九、建议(Suggestion)

| | |
|---|---|
| You may serve in turn. | 你们可以轮流发球。 |
| You can leave the racket on the table. | 你们可以把球拍放在桌上。 |
| Let's finish this part next time. | 让我们下次把这部分完成。 |
| Let's try serving. | 我们来试着发球。 |
| How about another block, Wang Hong? | 王红,再推挡一次好吗? |
| How about you coming out and trying? | 你出来试一试怎么样? |

| | |
|---|---|
| What about trying it once more? | 再来试一次好吗？ |
| I suggest that you learn the foot step first. | 我建议你先学习脚步。 |
| I think that you should finish the movement on your own. | 我认为你应该自己完成这个动作。 |
| You might as well be a demonstration now. | 你现在不妨示范一下。 |
| You might as well grasp the basic skills first. | 你们不妨先掌握基本技术。 |
| You can improve your physical fitness. | 你可以改善你的身体。 |
| Watch out! / Take care! / Be careful! | 当心！／小心！ |
| Watch your step. / Mind the step! | 留心脚下！ |
| Try not to lift your hand too high. | 不要把手抬得太高。 |
| Be sure and remember what you will have to do next. | 千万要记住你们接下来需要做的事情。 |
| Don't talk in class, ok? | 不要在课堂上说话，好吗？ |
| Please mind what I am going to tell you. | 请注意我要告诉你们的事情。 |
| Listen to me. | 听我讲。 |
| The purpose of the game is for you to develop agility. | 这个游戏的目的是培养你们的灵敏性。 |
| Keep trunk upright, with elbows slightly bent. | 保持躯干直立，肘微曲。 |
| Completely relax your muscles. | 完全放松你的肌肉。 |
| Turn waist to right. | 腰向右转。 |
| Lean trunk forward/backward. | 躯干向前/后倾斜。 |
| Stand still. | 站着别动。 |
| Jump up and down. | 上下跳。 |
| Shift weight forward. | 重心前移。 |
| Weight moves onto right/left leg. | 重心移至右/左腿。 |
| Power should be focused at wrist. | 手腕发力。 |
| Keep your body and mind relaxed. | 身心放松。 |
| Everybody please concentrate. | 大家请集中注意力。 |
| All of you concentrate! | 你们大家要注意了！ |
| Please concentrate your attention. | 请集中注意力。 |
| Be spirited, relax the whole body. | 精神饱满，全身放松。 |

| Be in high spirit. | 情绪高涨些。 |
| Raise your head. | 抬头。 |
| Look forward. | 向前看。 |

# 十、鼓励（Encouragement）

| Good！ | 好！ |
| Good job！ | 干得不错！ |
| Fine！ | 很好！ |
| Excellent！ | 优秀！ |
| That's right！ | 对了！ |
| That's correct！ | 对了！ |
| Well done！ | 做得很好！ |
| Right！ | 对！ |
| Quite right！ | 非常对！ |
| Quite good！ | 好极了！ |
| That's quite right！ | 非常好！ |
| That's very good/nice！ | 那很好！ |
| You did it well！ | 你做得很好！ |
| You have improved your table tennis skill. | 你已经提高了乒乓球技术。 |
| That's much better. | 好多了。 |
| You have make a lot of progress. | 你取得了很大进步。 |
| Your ready position is much better. | 你的准备姿势好一些了。 |
| Not exactly. Would you try it again？ | 不够准确，再做一次好吗？ |
| Good try，but not quite right. | 很好的尝试，但不完全正确。 |
| Almost right. | 差不多对了。 |
| Push stroke skill need improverment. | 推球技术需要改进。 |
| Take it easy！There is no need to hurry. | 别着急，不必急。 |
| Go on！Have a try. | 继续下去，试试看。 |
| Don't worry！I will help you. | 别担忧，我会帮助你。 |
| Never mind，you can do the action well. | 没关系，你能做好这个动作。 |

# 十一、总结（Summing-up）

| | |
|---|---|
| There are still five minutes left. | 还有五分钟。 |
| You will have to finish the drill in a minute. | 你们必须在一分钟内完成练习。 |
| I'm afraid it's time to finish now. | 恐怕现在该结束了。 |
| There's the bell, so we must stop working now. | 铃响了，所以我们现在必须停止工作。 |
| Stop now! You may have a rest. | 现在停止！你们可以休息一下。 |
| All right! You can finish now. | 好，你们现在可以完成了。 |
| That's all for today! Dismiss! | 今天就到这里！解散！ |
| I'd like to sum up the course in one sentence. | 我想用一句话概括这节课。 |
| I shall summarize what we have learnt today. | 我将概括一下我们今天所学的东西。 |
| Let me make a summary! Today we have learnt how to play push stroke. | 让我来做一个总结，今天我们学习了如何推球。 |
| To sum up, table tennis is important for all of us to keep fit. | 概括地说，乒乓球对我们大家保持健康很重要。 |
| I shall repeat what we have learnt this time. | 我重复一下这次学过的内容。 |
| Due to the time is up, I will point out the key movements of the serving. | 由于时间到了，我将指出发球的关键动作。 |
| Finally, I want to stress the following points. | 最后，我想强调下列要点。 |
| Your movement is still not quite correct. | 你们的动作还不太正确。 |
| Some of you haven't got perfect movements. | 有一些人动作还不够完美。 |
| You need some more practice with these actions. | 你需要把这些动作多做几遍。 |
| You have a very good serving skill. | 你的发球技术非常好。 |
| All of you have done a good job today. | 今天你们做得很好。 |
| You have done a good job at this part. | 你们这个部分学得不错。 |
| After class remember to take the racket. | 下课要记得带球拍。 |

Please remember what I said today. 请记住我今天讲的内容。

Don't forget your sports shoes next time. 下次别忘记你的运动鞋。

Please don't forget to bring the ball. 请别忘记把球带来。

What we shall learn next is looping. 下一次我们将学习拉弧圈球。

You should finish this part next Friday. 下周五要完成这个部分。

We'll go on with serve next class. Please get ready before class. 下次课我们继续学习发球。请在课前做好准备。

If you have any questions, we can discuss them later. 如果你们有什么问题，我们以后讨论。

I would like to make further explanations for you at anytime. 我愿意随时为你们做进一步的说明。

I don't think we've got time to let you practice. 我想现在我们没有时间让你们练习了。

We still have a couple of minutes left. 我们还有几分钟的时间。

Stay where you are for a moment, I have got something to say. 在原位上稍等一会儿，我有话要说。

What we have learnt today can be summarized as follows：first..., second... 今天我们学的主要内容可以归纳如下：第一，……；第二，……

I shall sum up the key points of the lessons. 我来总结本课的要点。

As time is limited, I only point out one： All of you have done a good job today. 由于时间有限，我仅说明一点：今天你们学得都不错。

# 第七章 裁判员临场操作与竞赛编排
# (Organization and arrangement of table tennis competition and referee's action during match)

## 一、裁判员临场操作程序(Referee on the spot operation procedure)

裁判员临场操作程序分为:赛前、赛中、赛后三个部分。

### (一)赛前(Before the match)

#### 1. 赛前准备(pre match preparation)

(1)报到(roll call)。裁判员:赛前 30 min 向裁判长报到。副裁判员:赛前 30 min 向裁判长报到,领取名牌及器材。

(2)挑球与检查(pick the ball and check)。裁判员:赛前 20 min,在指定区域挑球,检查球拍、服装和号码布,确定指导者。副裁判员:协助裁判员。

(3)记分表与比赛用球(score sheet and match ball)。裁判员:赛前 10 min 应拿到记分单及比赛用球。副裁判员:整理比赛用具。

(4)交流(communication)。裁判员:进入赛区前和副裁判员简短交流。副裁判员:与裁判员交流。

(5)排队(line up)。裁判员:在入口处排成一列,顺序是裁判员、运动员、副裁判员,裁判员左手拿记分单和球。副裁判员:与裁判员排成一列。

(6)入场(admission)。裁判员:①进入赛区执裁用品应放在口袋里,不能露在外面或者挂在脖子上;②迈着统一的步伐,直线行进;③到达台区后,转身走向球台端线处。副裁判员:同上。

①入场:①执裁用品,如笔、秒表、量网尺、红黄白牌不应露在外面;②手提包(私人物品)应放在指定的区域;③步伐稳健,轻快地摆臂,直线前进;④决不可跨越挡板,应在两个挡板挪开一个空隙。

②交流：应就谁控制练习时间、局与局间隔时间(副裁判员)和谁控制暂停时间(裁判员)及谁在暂停时放置暂停牌(副裁判员)达成一致。

**2. 到达比赛场地(arrive at the playing area)**

(1)到达(arrive)。裁判员：带队进入场地内，以立正姿势站在离球台端线偏右、约4 m处。副裁判员：应跟随裁判员进入场地，以立正姿势站在离球台端线偏左、约4 m处。

(2)介绍(introduce)。裁判员：名字被点到时向前迈一小步，然后向后一小步回到原来的位置。副裁判员：同上。

(3)站立(stand)。裁判员：在指定位置站立至少5 s。副裁判员：同上。

**3. 赛前程序(pre competition procedure)**

(1)练习前(before practice)。裁判员：①检查球拍(如果挑球时没有检查)；②检查运动服着色颜色；③检查运动员号码布；④单项比赛确定指导者；⑤用挑边器抽签、确定发球和方位；⑥指示副裁判员计练习时间；⑦完成记分单上相关信息的填写。副裁判员：①检查网高和张度；②将球台台面和地板清理干净；③将名牌摆好摆正；④将记分器复位到空白(如需要)；⑤如运动员到达或走近比赛场地、将记分器场分翻至0；⑥根据裁判员指示计练习时间。

(2)练习时(exercise time)。裁判员：坐在裁判椅上。副裁判员：坐在副裁判椅上。

(3)赛前宣告(pre game announcement)。裁判员：①用一种镇静的、不慌不忙的精确的语言宣告(宣告内容略)；②应尽力把每位运动员的名字念准。副裁判员：坐在副裁判椅上。

**4. 比赛开始(start of the game)**

裁判员：①"时间到"宣布发球；②指向发球方，同进注视接发球主是否准备好；③当发球方准备好，宣布"××发球，0比0"。

副裁判员：①当练习时间到，举起手臂宣布"时间到"；②将比分翻至0∶0；③启动秒表，比赛开始。

## (二)赛中(Match)

**1. 比赛过程中(during play)**

(1)手势(gesture)。裁判员：应用统一的手势。副裁判员：应用统一的手势。

（2）报分（call the score）。裁判员：报分清晰洪亮，使坐在教练席上的人能听到报分。

（3）计时（time）。裁判员：比赛计时或是指定副裁判员计时。副裁判员：根据裁判员指示，计比赛时间。

（4）发球（serve）。裁判员：监督并确保发球合法。注意发球秩序，发球擦网及双打发球时是否落在规定的区域内。副裁判员：①监督并确保发球合法；②注意发球秩序、发球擦网。

（5）行为（behaviour）。裁判员：监督并确保运动员的行为合法。副裁判员：裁判员出示黄牌后应将黄色标志物放在翻分器该运动员得分处。

（6）球拍（racket）。裁判员：在局与局之间，确保运动员的球拍放在球台上。副裁判员：坐在副裁判椅上。

（7）连续性（continuity）。裁判员：①不能在规定时间之外擦汗、暂停；②坚决劝阻诸如重复拍球、发球前长时间停顿、双打时长时间相互讨论等拖延比赛的行为。副裁判员：如果赛区内有人受伤流血，协同裁判员将赛区内所有血迹擦干净。

（8）场外指导（bench coaching）。裁判员：①监督并确保教练员的指导合法，在分与分之间和决胜局交换方位时，应转过头去监督双方的教练员是否指导；②当有非法指导时，第一次应出示黄牌警告非法指导者，第二次，出示红牌将其逐出比赛区域。副裁判员：①监督赛前商定的一名指导者；②必要时可提示裁判员注意。

（9）擦边和阻挡（edge and barrier）。裁判员：①注意球的运行方向和击球的一瞬间；②正确判断擦边球和阻挡。副裁判员：①正确判断阻挡；②决定处于比赛状态的球是否触及离他最近的比赛台面的上边缘。

（10）意外干扰（unexpected disturbance）。裁判员：比赛环境受到干扰，以致该回合结果可能受到影响，应立即暂停比赛，干扰消除后立即恢复比赛。如：外界球进入赛区，比赛球飞出赛区、球破裂、突发声响、灯光事故等。副裁判员：可对比赛环境受到意外干扰，该回合的结果有可能受到影响时进行判决；意外干扰发生时应立即停表，一旦消除，应及时恢复计时。

（11）暂停（time out）。裁判员：①应一方或双方要求，可在一场比赛中暂停一次，时间不超过1分钟；②暂停比赛，出示白牌；③启动秒表，计暂停时间；④应在要求暂停一方运动员（或双方要求暂停运动员）准备恢复比赛或时间满1分钟时继续比赛。副裁判员：①裁判员同意暂停，应立即停表；②将白牌（T牌）放在提出暂停要求一方（或双方）运动员的台区中线近端线一量网尺的距离，面向外；③恢复比赛时应拿走白牌（T 牌）；④将白牌放置在要求暂停一方（或双方）记分牌的得分旁；⑤比赛开始，恢复计时。

（12）轮换发球法（expedite system）。裁判员：①听到副裁判员宣布"时间到"，应立即中断比赛，并宣布从下一个发球开始按轮换发球法进行；②球处于比赛状态，由原发球员发球，不过未处于比赛状态，由前一回合接发球员发球；③听到副裁判员或指派的计数员报出"13"时，若该球合法还击，应判接发球方得 1 分。副裁判员：①一局比赛进行到 10 分钟仍未结束（比分已达到至少 18 分除外）应宣布"时间到"；②停止计时；③从下一个发球开始从 1～13 依次清晰地报出接发球员的击球次数。

（13）双打比赛（doubles match）。裁判员：①双打时应记住和在记分单上标明第一发球员和第一接发球员；②发、接不过次序若发现错误，应立即暂停比赛，纠正后继续比赛；③决胜局中，当一方先得 5 分时，接发球方应交换接发球次序；④如果裁判椅不够高，应该站立执裁。副裁判员：①注意发球、接发球次序变换，必要时给裁判员暗示；②决胜局交换方位时，及时停表和开表。

（14）宣布结束（announced the end）。裁判员：比赛结束，在记分单上填写完最后一局比分后，同时宣布比赛结果（"11 比×，某某以 3 比×胜"）。

## （三）赛后（After the match）

### 1. 赛后程序（post match procedure）

签名（autograph）。裁判员：如果裁判长要求，让运动员在记分单上签名。副裁判员：①返回局分和比分，记分器恢复为空白；②把球收好，将场地恢复到适当条件（若有名牌应取下）。

### 2. 裁判员退场（the referee exeunt）

（1）离场（exeunt）。裁判员：①与副裁判员在裁判椅前会合，裁判员在离出口处近的一方，排队退场；②左手拿记分单在副裁判员之前退场。副裁判员：①与裁判员在裁判椅前会合；②随裁判员身后退场。

（2）交记分单（hand over score sheet）。裁判员：确认记分单完整、准确后，将记分单直接交裁判长席。副裁判员：归还名牌及器材。

（3）就座观赛（just watch game）。裁判员、副裁判员：值裁后不应该在赛区内逗留或闲逛，如果要观看比赛，应在指定区域或观众席就座。

## （四）小结（Summary）

### 1. 统一着装（uniform dress）

凡出现在比赛区域的裁判员必须着统一制服。

### 2. 谈话得体（talk properly）

裁判员应避免在赛前、赛中、赛后对运动员评头论足。

裁判员应回答运动员疑问，或解释执法的依据，但决不挑起与比赛无关的话。

### 3. 注意形象（pay attention to image）

裁判员着统一制服时，应注意他们自己所代表的协会，特别是他们的行动将会给他们所有裁判员带来影响。

### 4. 尊重风俗（respect customs）

赛场内外，所有的裁判员都要尊重当地的风俗习惯。

### 5. 恪守规范（abide by the norm）

在任何情况下，裁判员不能让观众或媒体工作人员影响与自己和行为或官员的行为有关的事情。遇类似情况应直接报告裁判长或竞赛负责人。

### 6. 裁判常用表格标准样式（referee's match score sheet）

乒乓球比赛国际标准用记分单见附录一、附录二。

# 二、乒乓球竞赛组织与编排（Organization and arrangement of table tennis competition）

## （一）乒乓球竞赛项目和方法（Table tennis events and methods）

### 1. 竞赛项目（competition project）

男、女团体；男、女单打；男、女双打；混合双打（mixed doubles）共七项。

### 2. 竞赛方法（competition method）

团体：一场团体比赛一般由五盘三胜组成，每盘五局三胜，每局11分制。

| 比赛次序 | 主队 | | 客队 |
|---|---|---|---|
| ① | A | — | X |
| ② | B | — | Y |
| ③ | C | — | Z |
| ④ | A | — | Y |
| ⑤ | B | — | X |

介绍：北京奥运会团体赛制

出场顺序为：① A—X；② B—Y；③ A（B）/C—X（Y）/Z；④ B（A）—Z；⑤C—Y（X）

（1）每场团体赛打五盘，第三盘为双打，其余四盘是单打；

（2）每队只有 3 名队员报名参加奥运会，这 3 人在团体赛上都要出场，每名队员最多只能参加两盘比赛（两盘单打，或者一盘单打一盘双打）；

（3）第三盘双打比赛的人选，可以在前两盘单打比赛结束之后由教练临时决定，但不能由前两盘已经出场的两名单打选手配对；

（4）赛前双方抽签确定主客队，主队的第四盘单打由未参加双打的队员出场，客队的第四单打由未参加前两场单打的队员出场。

在此赛制下，双方的第四、五盘单打不会重复第一、二盘的对阵，如果参赛双方打满 5 盘，那么 3 名球员每个人都要出场两次。

单项分为单打和双打：

单打：单循环（五局三胜 match best of 5 games）。

单淘汰（七局四胜 match best of 7 games）。

双打：一般均采用五局三胜。

## （二）基本比赛方法（Basic match method）

### 1. 循环赛（round-robin）

（1）定义。

单循环：参赛单位相互之间均要轮流比赛一次（主客场制为双循环赛，轮流比赛两次）。

（2）轮数和场数的计算。

一轮（参赛单位均出场比赛一次包括轮空）

轮数等于单数或双数 – 1

即：5 队 = 5 轮，6 队 = 6 – 1 = 5 轮

$$场数 = \frac{参赛队数 \times (参赛队数 - 1)}{2}$$

即：$\frac{6(6-1)}{2} = \frac{30}{2} = 15$

（3）比赛次序的确定。

介绍"1号位不动的逆时针轮转法"。

例：5队（人）循环

表 7 – 1

| 轮次 | 一 | 二 | 三 | 四 | 五 |
|------|------|------|------|------|------|
| 轮转方法 | 1—0 | 1—5 | 1—4 | 1—3 | 1—2 |
| | 2—5 | 0—4 | 5—3 | 4—2 | 3—0 |
| | 3—4 | 2—3 | 0—2 | 5—0 | 4—5 |

　　规则 3.7.5.5[①]——经仲裁委员会许可除外，如果小组预选将选出一人或一队，该小组的最后一场比赛应在小组排列第一或第二位的选手或队之间进行；如果小组预选将选出两人或两队，该小组的最后一场比赛应该在小组排列第二和第三位的运动员或队之间进行，并依此类推。

（4）比赛名次的确定。

根据所获得的分数决定（2，1，0）。

　　①得分相同的队应先计算他们之间场次分数，再计算胜负比率（场、局、分）；

　　②计算得分再相同的成员，应将已决定出名次的小组成员的比赛成绩删除；

　　③不能决定某些队（人）的名次时，将由抽签来决定。

　　例：

---

①　中国乒乓球协会. 乒乓球竞赛规则［M］. 北京：人民体育出版社，2016.

表 7 – 2

|  | A | B | C | D | E | F | 积分 | 计算 | 名次 |
|---|---|---|---|---|---|---|---|---|---|
| A | ※ | 3:1 | 2:3 | 2:3 | 0:3 | 3:1 | 7 4 | 3 5/4 | 4 |
| B | 1:3 | ※ | 3:0 | 2:3 | 1:3 | 3:2 | 7 4 | 3 4/3 | 3 |
| C | 3:2 | 0:3 | ※ | 2:3 | 2:3 | 3:0 | 7 4 | 3 3/5 | 5 |
| D | 3:2 | 3:2 | 3:2 | ※ | 0:3 | w−0:3 | 7 6 |  | 2 |
| E | 3:2 | 3:1 | 3:2 | 3:0 | ※ | 3:1 | 10 |  | 1 |
| F | 1:3 | 2:3 | 0:3 | 3:w−0 | 1:3 | ※ | 6 |  | 6 |

请计算：
①组内积分（E 为 1 名，F 为 6 名）。
②相同积分的四队之间比赛的积分（D 为 2 名）。
③A、B、C 三队之间比赛的积分（仍相同）。
④A、B、C 三队之间比赛的胜负比率（A5/4 为 4 名，B4/3 为 3 名，C3/5 为 5 名）。

**2. 淘汰赛（knockout match）**

（1）定义和特点。
将所有参赛选手顺序排列成一定的比赛秩序后，由相邻的两名参赛者之间进行比赛，败者被淘汰出局，失去继续比赛的资格；而胜者被保留，进入下一轮继续以相同的方式进行比赛，直到淘汰剩最后一名参赛者。（最后未被淘汰的参赛者即为这次比赛的冠军）
优点：
①比赛双方具有强烈的对抗性和竞争性，非胜亦败，不受第三方影响也不影响第三方。
②短时间内可以安排大量的比赛（竞赛效率高）。
③比赛逐步走向高潮，趋向高水平激烈比赛。
缺点：
①合理性差，打一场胜一片，名次分布有规律。淘汰赛名次分布的规律：

冠、亚军必产生于两个不同的 1/2 区；第 3、4 名必然产生于两个不同的 1/2 区中没有冠、亚军的另外两个 1/4 区，也就是说前四名必然产生于四个不同的1/4 区；第 5~8 名(或四个并列第五名)又必产生于四个不同的 1/4 区中没有第 1~4 名的另外的四个 1/8 区，也就是说前八名必然产生于八个不同的 1/8 区；这在理论上是无法证明的，所以也就是不合理的。

②机遇性强，不同的比赛秩序不同的比赛结果。

③不完整性，要求参赛单位数为 2 的某次幂。

(2)号码位置数的选择。

2 的乘方数：8，16，32，64 等。

(3)轮数和场数的计算。

轮数 = 乘方数的幂

即：32 = 2 的 5 次幂 = 5 轮

场数 = 参赛队数 − 1    即：34 = 34 − 1 = 33

(4)附加赛。

前八名附加赛排名表(见附录四)。

**3. 综合制( comprehensive system )**

综合制在实际比赛中一般都采取先循环后淘汰，具体做法是：先抽签进行分组，循环比赛后根据积分取出各小组前 1~2 或 1~4 名交叉淘汰(结合附加赛)决出名次。

## (三)种子、轮空、抢号(Seed，Bye，Extra match for the No. )

### 1. 种子( seed )

(1)数目：分组循环赛根据组数设立，淘汰赛必须是 2 的乘方数。

(2)位置：分组循环赛均匀分布在各组，淘汰赛均匀分布在各区(顶部和底部，要求用"跟种子规律"熟记 8 个种子位置)。

例如：在 16 人的单淘汰比赛中，上次比赛的前 8 名被列为种子，分别用以下数字表示

第一名：①    第二名：②    第三名：③    第四名：④

第五名：⑤    第六名：⑥    第七名：⑦    第八名：⑧

在运动员没有到场抽签的情况下可以做如下安排(见下图)：

如正式比赛除第一名和第二名分别位列 1 和 16 外，8 和 9 应由第三名和第四名抽入，5 和 12 应由第五名和第六名抽入，4 和 13 应由第七名和第八名

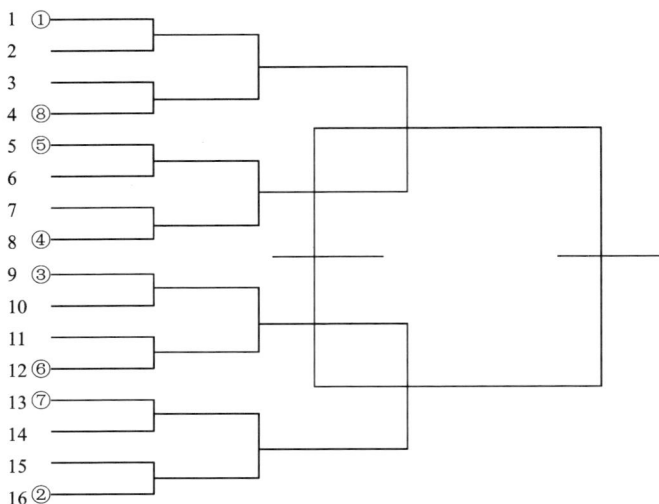

图 7 – 1　16 个位置的 8 个种子位置（seed place）图

抽入。

**2. 轮空和抢号（Bye and Extra match for the No.）**

（1）轮空数 = 号码位置数 – 参赛人数

抢号数 = 参赛人数 – 号码位置数

（2）轮空和抢号位置。

种子位置数为单数时——+1

种子位置数为双数时—— – 1

## （四）抽签和编排（Draw and layout）

**1. 抽签原则（draw principle）**

种子选手合理分开，最后相遇；

同单位选手合理分开，最后相遇。

**2. 抽签方法（draw method）**

（1）淘汰赛抽签实例（knockout draw examples）。

有 12 个单位的 60 名选手参加乒乓球女子单打比赛，各参赛单位人数分别为：

A 队：4 人　　　B 队：6 人　　　C 队：8 人　　　D 队：1 人

E 队：4 人　　　F 队：7 人　　　G 队：5 人　　　H 队：2 人

I 队：3 人　　　J 队：8 人　　　K 队：4 人　　　L 队：8 人

比赛采用淘汰制，设 8 名种子：

第 1 号种子：A1

第 2 号种子：C1

第 3～4 号种子：C2、A2

第 5～8 号种子：E1、C3、K1、E2

单淘汰赛的抽签分为种子运动员抽签和非种子运动员抽签两部分。首先对种子运动员进行抽签，然后进行非种子运动员抽签。

（2）种子运动员抽签（seed athlete draw）。

种子运动员采用分级分批抽签一次定位：

①确定第 1 和第 2 号种子的号码位置。根据乒乓球竞赛规则规定，第 1 号种子 A1 进上半区顶部即 1 号位置。2 号种子 C1 进入下半区底部即 64 号位置。

②确定第 3、4 号种子的号码位置。第 3～4 号种子应用抽签的办法分别抽入 32、33 号位置，由于 A1 已进入 1 号位置，同单位的 A2 应抽入 A1 不在的另一个 1/2 区即进入 33 号位置。同理，C2 进入 32 号位置。

③最后确认 5～8 号种子的位置。由于 C1、C2 已分别定位于第 4、第 2 个 1/4 区，C3 只能抽入 C1、C2 所不在的第 1、第 3 个 1/4 区。设 C3 随机抽入第 3 和 1/4 区，剩下三个第 5～8 个种子中，有两个种子是同单位的，E1、E2 他们必须分别抽入第 1 个 1/2 区和第 2 个 1/2 区，而下半部还剩一个种子位置，在第 4 个 1/4 区，E1、E2 必须有 1 人进入第 4 个 1/4 区，设 E2 抽入第 4 个 1/4 区即 49 号位置。E1 抽入上半区的第 1 或第 2 个 1/4 区，设 E1 抽入 16 号位置。最后一个 5－8 号种子 K1，方能进入第 2 个 1/4 区的 17 号位置。

### 3. 编排方法（layout method）

即确定全部比赛的日期、时间和台号。

编排常识：

（1）团体比赛安排 90～120 min。

（2）单项比赛安排 15～30 min。

（3）一张球台比赛总量：每节 2 个团体或 7～10 场单项比赛。

（4）一队、一人比赛总量：每天一队最多打 2～4 个团体；每天一人最多打 5～7 场单项比赛。

# 附录一　单项记分单
# （INDIVIDUAL MATCH SCORE SHEET）

**International Table Tennis Federation**
Sun International
**2016 World Junior Table Tennis Championships**
30 Nov - 7 Dec 2016, Cape Town (RSA)

| 单项记分单 INDIVIDUAL MATCH SCORE SHEET | | | Match ID | **171** |
|---|---|---|---|---|

| 项目Event: | U13 Girls' Singles | 阶段Stage: | Group 13 - 3rd Rd | 5-Jan | 15:50 | Table 15 |
|---|---|---|---|---|---|---|

| | | Serv. | Y | YR1 | YR2 | TO | Games | | TO | Y | YR1 | YR2 | Serv. | | |
|---|---|---|---|---|---|---|---|---|---|---|---|---|---|---|---|
| **Player A/AB** | Name of Coach | | | | | | 11 | 1st | 5 | | | | | ✖ | Name of Coach |
| | **201** | | | | | | 5 | 2nd | 11 | | | | | | **252** |
| | **AUS** | | ✖ | | | ✖ | 13 | 3rd | 11 | | ✖ | | | | **FRA** |
| | **MORTON Darcie** | | | | | | 11 | 4th | 7 | ✖ | | ✖ | | | **GUISNEL Oceane** |
| | | | | | | | | 5th | | | | | | | |
| | **3** | | | | | | ✖ | 6th | ✖ | | | | | **1** | |
| | | | | | | | ✖ | 7th | ✖ | | | | | | |

| Winner: | Number 201 | Name MORTON Darcie (AUS) | | If wirtten report attached please mark here. |
|---|---|---|---|---|

| T-shirt color | P1 | **Red** | P2 | **Black** | Racket Checked Before Match | P1 | **Y** | P2 | **N** |
|---|---|---|---|---|---|---|---|---|---|

| Ball Selected | P1 | **Y** | P2 | **N** | | | |
|---|---|---|---|---|---|---|---|

| A/AB SIGNATURE | | | X/XY SIGNATURE |
|---|---|---|---|

判罚记录Warning/Penalties:　　252: Y - delaying the game.　201: Y- misbehaviour　252: YR1 misbehaviour

| Umpire 1: | Numbr Name | Assoc. | Signature Umpires: | only umpire to sign |
|---|---|---|---|---|
| Umpire 2: | Numbr Name | Assoc. | Validation Referee: | leave blank for referee |

Serv.=Server in the 1st game　　　　Y =Yellow
YR1 =Yellow/Red/1 point　　　　　　YR2 =Yellow/Red/2 point
TO =Time Out

# 附录二　团体记分单
# ( TEAM MATCH SCORE SHEET )

**International Table Tennis Federation**
Sun International
2016 World Junior Table Tennis Championships
30 Nov - 7 Dec 2016, Cape Town (RSA)

团体记分单 TEAM MATCH SCORE SHEET

| 场次号 | 组别项目 | 日期 | 阶段 | 组别 | 轮次 | 开始时间 | 结束时间 | 时间 | 台号 |
|---|---|---|---|---|---|---|---|---|---|
| 86 | Junior Boys Teams | 3/12 | 1 | A | 3 | 09:30 | 10:50 | 09:30 | 4 |

| ABC | BELGIUM | 对 | FRANCE | XYZ |
|---|---|---|---|---|
| ABC队长/教练 | Name of Coach | | Name of Coach | XYZ队长/教练 |

**A — DARCIS Thibaut 0 vs CASSIN Alexandre 3 (X)**

| S | Y | YR1 | YR2 | TO | 每局比分 | | | TO | Y | YR1 | YR2 | S |
|---|---|---|---|---|---|---|---|---|---|---|---|---|
| × | | | | | 8 | 1 | 11 | | | | | |
| | | | | | 6 | 2 | 11 | | | | | |
| | | | | | 5 | 3 | 11 | | | | | |
| | | | | | | 4 | | | | | | |
| | | | | | | 5 | | | | | | |

**B — DEVOS Laurens 2 vs BERTRAND Irvin 3 (Y)**

| S | Y | YR1 | YR2 | TO | 每局比分 | | | TO | Y | YR1 | YR2 | S |
|---|---|---|---|---|---|---|---|---|---|---|---|---|
| | | | | | 11 | 1 | 6 | | | | | × |
| | | | | | 10 | 2 | 12 | × | | | | |
| | | | | | 3 | 3 | 11 | | | | | |
| | | | | × | 11 | 4 | 9 | × | | | | |
| | | | | | 8 | 5 | 11 | | | | | |

**C — CNUDDE Florian 3 vs SEYFRIED Joe 1 (Z)**

| S | Y | YR1 | YR2 | TO | 每局比分 | | | TO | Y | YR1 | YR2 | S |
|---|---|---|---|---|---|---|---|---|---|---|---|---|
| × | | | | | 11 | 1 | 8 | | | | | |
| | | | | | 6 | 2 | 11 | | | | | |
| | | | | × | 11 | 3 | 9 | | | | | |
| | | | | | 11 | 4 | 6 | | | | | |

**A — DARCIS Thibaut 3 vs BERTRAND Irvin 2 (Y)**

| S | Y | YR1 | YR2 | TO | 每局比分 | | | TO | Y | YR1 | YR2 | S |
|---|---|---|---|---|---|---|---|---|---|---|---|---|
| × | | | | | 11 | 1 | 4 | | | | | |
| | | | | | 15 | 2 | 13 | | | | | |
| | | | | | 8 | 3 | 11 | | | | | |
| | | | | | 6 | 4 | 11 | | | | | |
| | | | | × | 11 | 5 | 9 | × | | | | |

**B — DEVOS Laurens 0 vs CASSIN Alexandre 3 (X)**

| S | Y | YR1 | YR2 | TO | 每局比分 | | | TO | Y | YR1 | YR2 | S |
|---|---|---|---|---|---|---|---|---|---|---|---|---|
| | | | | | 10 | 1 | 12 | | | | | × |
| | × | × | | | 10 | 2 | 12 | × | | | | |
| | | | | | 6 | 3 | 11 | | | | | |
| | | | | | | 4 | | | | | | |
| | | | | | | 5 | | | | | | |

| | 队名 | 场 分 | | 队名 | |
|---|---|---|---|---|---|
| ABC | BELGIUM | 2 | 3 | FRANCE | XYZ |

| 获胜队 | FRANCE | 有说明的问题做记号 |
|---|---|---|

| ABC队长签名 | DARCIS Thibaut | BERTRAND Irvin | XYZ队长签名 |
|---|---|---|---|

| 裁判员1 | Number　Name | Assoc. | 裁判员签字 | only umpire to sign |
|---|---|---|---|---|
| 裁判员2 | Number　Name | Assoc. | 裁判长签字 | leave blank for referee |

# 附录三　团体排名表
## （Team Order List）

××××××××赛

### 团体排名表
### Team Order List

| 项目<br>Event | 对阵双方<br>Team | 日期<br>Date | 场次号<br>Match ID | 阶段<br>Stage | 轮次<br>Round | 组别<br>Group | 时间<br>Time | 台号<br>Table |
|---|---|---|---|---|---|---|---|---|
| | | | | | | | | |

| A/B/C | X/Y/Z | 队名 | 号码 |
|---|---|---|---|
| | | 运动员1 | |
| | | 运动员2 | |
| | | 运动员3 | |
| | | 运动员4 | |
| | | 运动员5 | |
| 队长签名 / Captain's signature: | | | |

| 其他信息填写 |
|---|
| 服装主体颜色 |
| 颜色： |
| 教练席位选择（面向球网） |
| 席位： |
| 备注： |

---

××××××××赛

### 团体排名表
### Team Order List

| 项目<br>Event | 对阵双方<br>Team | 日期<br>Date | 场次号<br>Match ID | 阶段<br>Stage | 轮次<br>Round | 组别<br>Group | 时间<br>Time | 台号<br>Table |
|---|---|---|---|---|---|---|---|---|
| | | | | | | | | |

| A/B/C | X/Y/Z | 队名 | 号码 |
|---|---|---|---|
| | | 运动员1 | |
| | | 运动员2 | |
| | | 运动员3 | |
| | | 运动员4 | |
| | | 运动员5 | |
| 队长签名 / Captain's signature: | | | |

| 其他信息填写 |
|---|
| 服装主体颜色 |
| 颜色： |
| 教练席位选择（面向球网） |
| 席位： |
| 备注： |

# 附录四 "八强"附加赛排名表
## ( List of Top Eight Playoffs)

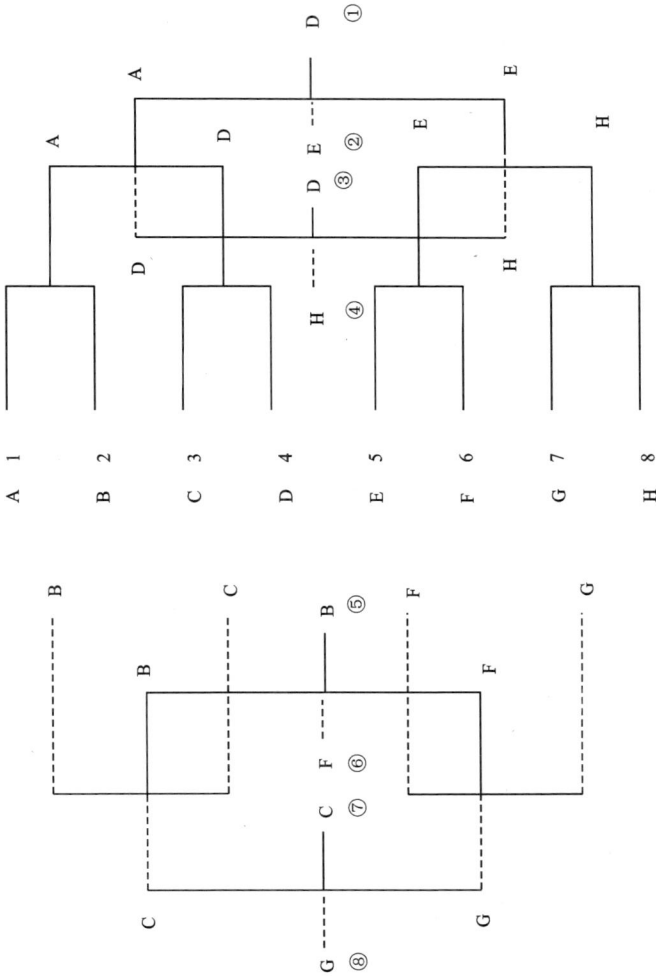

决1~8名

说明：———— 实线表示每场比赛位置 ----- 虚线表示每场比赛的负者
1234 5678表示比赛名次 ABCDEFGH表示参赛运动员 ①②③④⑤⑥⑦⑧表示比赛名次
实线表示每场比赛的胜者

# 附录五　乒乓球常用汉英专业词汇
# （Commonly used Chinese-English vocabulary on table tennis）

## 一、发球（Serve）

上旋：topspin

侧旋球：sidespin

右侧旋：right sidespin

左侧旋：left sidespin

右侧上旋：right side topspin

左侧上旋：left side topspin

左侧下旋：left side backspin

发球：serve, service

发球员：server

重发球：let

蹲踞式发球：squatting service

发不转球：knuckle service, serve without spin

发上旋球：topspin service

发下旋球：backspin service

发侧旋球：sidespin service

发平击球：flat service

发正手上旋球：forehand topspin service

发正手下旋球：forehand backspin service

发反手上旋球：backhand topspin service

发反手下旋球：backhand backspin service

发加转球：heavy spin serve

合法发球：good service

接球失误：missed receive

发球失误：missed serve, lose one's serve

发球落网：fall

发球触网：net ball，service touching the net

发球得分：service ace，serve point

发短球：short serve

发球未触及本区台面：volleyed service

发近台(削)球：short cut service

发直线球：straight along the table service

发球犯规：fault

发球权：right to serve

底线球：end-line shot，deep ball

不转弧线球：dummy loop

高抛式发球：high-toss serve

无遮挡发球：no-hiding serve

不转球：no spin/without spin

高抛球：throw a high ball

抛球：throw the ball

接球：reception，treat

接发球：return of service

摩擦球：brush the ball

不过网的球：fall

擦网好球：net in

擦网出界：net out

奔球：force contact serve

正手发转与不转：forehand spin or non-spin serve

反手发转与不转球：backhand spin or non-spin serve

正手发左侧上旋球：forehand left topspin with sidespin serve

正手发左侧下旋球：forehand left backspin with sidespin serve

反手发右侧上旋球：backhand right topspin with sidespin serve

反手发右侧下旋球：backhand right backspin with sidespin serve

反手发急下旋球：backhand fast and heavy backspin

逆旋转发球：reverse-spin serve

## 二、推挡(Block)

正手挡球：forehand block

反手挡球：backhand block

推球：block

加力推：accentuated block

猛烈推挡：hard block shot

反手斜线推挡：backhand cross-court block

平击：flat stroke

挡球回击：block return

推挡回击：push return

平挡球：flat block

推下旋球：backspin block

减力挡：cushion block

快推球：fast block

反手快拨：backhand quick block

推侧旋球：sidespin block

## 三、攻球（Attack）

正手：forehand

对攻：counter attack

反手对攻：backhand counter attack

直拍近台快攻：close-to-table pen-hold grip fast attack

正手反攻：forehand counter attack

正手击球：forehand stroke

正手进攻：forehand attack

近攻：close attack

长攻：far attack

平抽球：flat drive

正手快攻：forehand fast attack

正手远攻：forehand far attack

反手攻球：backhand attack

正手拉接：forehand attack return

正手连续攻球：forehand drive continuously

正手连续进攻：continuous drive with forehand and backhand

中台正手攻球：middle court forehand attack stroke

拦击：volley

连击：double hit

连续进攻：continuous smashes

两面攻：attack on both sides，two-winged attack

猛击：slam

猛扣：flat hit

侧身步：sideway step

侧身抢攻：sideway attack

侧身正手攻球：sideway forehand attack

大力扣杀：hammer drives

扣杀：smash

杀高球：smash a high ball

反手抖腕：backhand flick

反手击球：backhand stroke

反手扣杀：backhand smash

反手快攻：backhand fast attack

反手突击：backhand assault stroke

反手远攻：backhand far attack

反手直拨：backhand straight stroke

反击对攻：backhand drive and counter drive

发球抢攻：attack after service

发球抢位：lifted drive after service

放高球：lob

防守型打法：defensive play

快速旋转打法：speed-and-spin play

快带：fast bringing

快速攻杀：quick smash

推挡变线：change direction of block stroke

搓中突击：assault while pushing stroke

长短结合(的)打法：long and short play

长攻短吊相结合：combine long attack with drop shots

攻削结合：combination of attack and chop

近台快攻：close-table fast attack

近台反攻：close-table counter attack

抢攻：attack in advance

推挡侧身抢攻：sideway attack after block

左推右攻：backhand block with forehand attack

远台长攻：back court long attack

远台打法：back court play

远台防守：back court defence

远台防守反攻：far defence with counter attack

正手快点：forehand flip

反手快点：backhand flip

正手快带：forehand slightly force brush contact against drive

反手快带：backhand slightly force brush contact against drive

正手突击：forehand assault

正手中远台攻球：forehand drive off-table court

反手中远台攻球：backhand drive off-table court

正手杀高球：forehand smash lob

正手放高球：forehand lob

正手滑板球：forehand fake drive

侧身正手攻球：forehand drive in sideway step

直拍反手攻球：backhand attack in pen-hold grip

## 四、拉球（Topspin stroke）

弧圈球：loop

加转弧圈球：high spin loop drive

假弧圈球：dummy loop

拉球（上旋球）：topspin stroke

拉弧圈球：drive stroke

拉长短球：long and shot lifted balls

拉强旋转弧圈球：lift heavy-spin loop

前冲弧圈球：accelerated loop，fast loop drive

高调弧圈球：high loop

反手拉球：backhand topspin stroke

反手弧圈球：backhand loop

正手快拉：forehand fast topspin stroke

反手快拉：backhand fast topspin stroke

拉加转弧圈球：lift heavy loop

拉前冲弧圈球：lift accelerated loop

正手拉侧旋弧圈球：forehand sidespin loop

反手拉弧圈球：backhand lift loop

反手反撕弧圈球：backhand force brush against loop

直拍反手拉弧圈球：pen-hold grip backhand loop drive

反手拧拉：backhand twist topspin stroke

## 五、搓球（Push）

慢搓：slowly push

快搓：fast push

搓转与不转：spin or non-spin push

搓侧旋球：sidespin push

搓球摆短：drop shot push

正手削球：forehand chop

反手削球：backhand chop

搓中突击：sudden drive while exchanging pushes

## 六、战术（Tactics）

推攻战术：push and attack tactics

拉攻战术：topspin-stroke and drive tactics

削中反攻战术：chop and counter attack tactics

以削为主的战术：main tactics for chop

发球抢攻战术：attack after service tactics

接发球抢攻战术：receive attack tactics

搓攻战术：push and attack tactics

## 七、步法（Footwork）

单步：one step

滑步、并步：side step

交叉步：cross step

小碎步：quick short step

跳步：hop step

侧身步：sideway step

## 八、综合（Synthesis）

国际乒乓球联合会（ITTF）：International Table Tennis Federation

国际乒乓球赛：International Table Tennis Challenge

世界乒乓球锦标赛：World Table Tennis Championships

世界杯：World Cup

亚洲乒乓球锦标赛：Asian Table Tennis Championships

亚洲乒乓球联合会：Asian Table Tennis Federation

亚洲乒乓球联盟：Asian Table Tennis Union

亚洲杯：Asian Cup

欧洲乒乓球联盟（ETTU）：Europe Table Tennis Union

英国乒乓球协会：English Table Tennis Association

美国乒乓球协会（USTTA）：United States Table Tennis Association

日本乒乓球协会（JTTA）：Japan Table Tennis Association

反手打对方台角：backhand corner

反手直线球：back straight

连续对打：sustained rally

挥拍：swing

挥拍的幅度：amplitude of swing

挥拍路线：path of swing

挥拍速度：speed of swing

回球失误：make a fault return

向前挥臂：swing the arm forward

向前挥拍：forward swing

快准狠变：speed, accuracy, aggressiveness and variation

削攻结合型运动员：chop and attack player

防守型选手：defensive player

攻击式选手：attacking player

混合双打运动员：mixed-doubles player

全能型选手：all-around player

近台防守型选手：close table defensive player

凶狠弧圈型打法选手：power looper

同伴：partner

下旋：backspin, underspin

急球：fast ball

急推球：quick return

擦边球：edge ball

中路球：middle ball

界内球：inside ball

追身球：bodyline ball

多球训练：multi-ball practice

正面：front

正确执拍：orthodox grip

非执拍手：free hand

执拍手：racket hand

直拍握法：pen-hold grip

横拍握法：shake-hand grip

左手执拍者：left-hander

右手执拍者：right-hander

攻击点：attack point

攻击型打法：offensive play

乒乓球外交：ping-pong diplomacy

抖腕：shake the wrist

击球：stroke

击球部位：striking spot on the ball

击球出界：hit off the table

击球次序：order of play

打法：play

击触网球：catch a net

控制落点：control placement

深握：deep grip，strong grip

台内阻挡：interface

站位：position

站位次序：order of position

# 九、器材和场地（Equipment and court）

球：ball

软球：soft ball

硬球：hard ball

赛璐珞(乒乓球)：celluloid

球拍：bat，paddle，racket

木：wood

拍柄：handle

拍面：face of racket

球拍反面：reverse side of racket

球拍套：racket case

球拍底板：blade

硬胶球拍：hard glue racket

反胶球拍：reversed glue racket

双面胶球拍：double glue racket

橡胶拍：rubber bat

长胶球拍：long glue racket

海绵：sponge

胶皮清洁器：rubber cleaner

覆盖物：covering

胶皮：gum

反胶(套胶)：inverted rubber

正胶：short pimps rubber

海绵胶：sponge rubber

合成胶：synthetic rubber

颗粒胶：pimpled rubber

防弧胶：anti-spin rubber

正胶海绵拍：outward pimpled rubber

反胶海绵拍：inward pimpled rubber

挡板：barriers，surround(s)，blocking board

发球正中线：serve the midline

发球员的右半边：server's right half court

球台端线：front edge of table

计分器：score indicator

网：net

网架：net brace

网柱：pole，support

比赛（场）：match

范围：range

比赛场区：playing area

比赛厅：playing hall

台面：playing surface

近台：close to table

中台：middle court

远台：far from the table

全台：full court

右半台：right half court

左半区：left half court

接球员的右半区：receiver's right half court

接球员的左半区：receiver's left half court

# 十、裁判用语（Terms for referee）

裁判长：referee

裁判组长（主裁判）：chief umpire

副裁判长：deputy referee

裁判员：umpire

检录长：chief recorder

司线员：line umpire

检查员：inspector

教练员：coach

运动员：player

发球员：server

接球员：receiver

单打：singles

双打：doubles

男子单打：men's singles

男子双打：men's doubles

男子团体：men's team

女子单打：women's singles

女子双打：women's doubles

混合双打：mixed doubles

女子团体：women's team

选拔赛：selection league tournament

半决赛：semi-final

配对（双打）：pairing

团体比赛：team games

局胜制：best of games

11 分制：11 point scoring system

决胜球：deciding ball

决胜局（比赛）：deciding game

种子选手：seeds

轮换发球法：expedite system

主队队员抽签代号：A B C

客队队员抽签代号：X Y Z

得分：point，score

二平：thirty all

各胜一局：one game each

换发球：change service

交换方位：change ends

交换场地：change sides

合法还击：good return

选边和发球：choice of ends and service

擦边球：edge ball

擦网：touched net

挑边：toss

警告：warning

静止：stationary

开始：beginning

停：stop

暂停：pause

选择：select

新的：new

失误：fault

拦击：volley

连击：double hit

上边缘：top edge

练习两分钟：practice two minutes

手扶台（面）：hand on table

球台移动：move table

手指转球：finger spin

有效发球：good service

准备，发球：ready，serve

边线：side line

端线：end line

中线：center line

球破裂：broken ball

次序错了：wrong order

轮换发球：alternate serve

换发球（单打）：change of service

出界：out

触网：touch net

触网球（发球）：let-ball

触网球（中间）：net-ball

触网柱：touch pole

时间限制：time limit

三局两胜：best of three games

×以，领先：× leads，games to

×以，获胜：× match to，games to

还有一分钟（离开局）：one minute left

上场：ready to play system

淘汰制：knock-out

循环赛：round robin

局：game

向上：upwards

近似垂直：approximately vertical

下降的：descending

看得见：visible

之上：above

之下：below

之后：behind

越过或绕过：over or around

局点：game point

决胜点（赛点）：match point

国际裁判长：international referee（IR）

国际裁判：international umpire（IU）

中立裁判：neutral umpire

记球员：stroke counter

计时员：timekeeper

一场比赛开始：beginning of the match

比赛之连续性：continuity of play

有怀疑的球：doubtful service

平坦及张开的手心：flat and open palm

不合法发球：illegal service

违反规章：breach of regulations

被禁止：forbidden

不合法：illegal

侵犯：infringe to

规则的诠释：interpretation of rules

发球规则：service law

时限：time limit

连跳：double bounce

解释：explanation

非持拍手触及台面：free hand on the table

×胜此局，11 比 7：game to ×，11：7

不能长时间中断：No long breaks！

尚未准备好：no ready

局数一比一：one game each

在球台之上：over the table

球员错误：wrong player

方位错误：wrong side

×以局数二比一领先：× leads 2 games to 1

×发球：× to serve

罚分：penalty points

驳回诉讼：dismissal

取消资格：disqualification

就事实所为之抗议：question of fact

裁判长报告：referee's report

报告裁判长：report to referee

行为不端：misbehave

不良行为：misbehaviour

冒犯的行为：offensive behaviour

五局三胜：match best of five games

七局四胜：match best of seven games

# 附录六 乒乓球专业英英词汇
## （Table Tennis English Vocabulary）

**All – around attacker**（全面型打法选手）

A player who can adjust his game to take advantage of an opponent´s weaknesses.

**Antispin**（防弧胶皮）

An inverted rubber sheet with a slick surface that produces mostly low – spin returns. It usually has a dead sponge underneath and is used mostly for defensive shots. Also known as anti.

**attacking chopper**（削球打法选手）

A player who uses a style of play based on mixing defensive chopping strokes with strong forehand topspin strokes.

**Backhand**（反手）

A stroke executed with the racket to the left elbow for a right – handed player, the reserve for a left – handed player.

**Backspin**（下旋）

A type of spin used mostly on defensive shots. To produce backspin, the racket contacts the ball below its center with a downward, chopping action. While the ball is traveling forward, it rotates back toward the player who hit it. This is also called underspin.

**Blade**（底板）

The wood part of the racket without covering.

**Block**（挡）

A quick, off – the – bounce return of an aggressive drive executed by holding the racket in the ball's path.

**Chop**（削接）

A defensive return of a drive or topspin with backspin, usually done well away from the table(see backspin).

**Chop block**（削球）

A block in which the racket moves downward at contact to create backspin.

**Close – to – the – table defender**（近台防守型打法选手）

A player who uses a style of play based on defensive blocking to force errors from the opponent.

**Counterdrive**（对攻）

A drive made against a drive.

**Counterdriver**（对攻型打法选手）

A player who uses a style of play based on consistent counterdriving from both backhand and forehand.

**Countersmash**（扣杀对扣杀）

To smash a smash(see smash).

**Countertopspin**（counterloop）（反拉弧圈球）

To loop a loop (see loop).

**Crosscourt**（对角）

From corner to corner diagonally .

**Default**（因犯规取消资格）

Being disqualified from a match for any reason.

### Double – motion serve（假动作发球）

A deceptive serve in which the server makes two quick motions at the ball in an attempt to disguise where contact is made on the ball.

### Down the line（边线）

Along one side of the table, parallel to the side lines.

### Drive stroke（攻球）

A fast, attacking stroke that carries minimum topspin.

### Drop shot（摆短）

A ball that drops short over the net so that the opponent has trouble reaching it; often used to return a short serve or when an opponent is back from the table.

### Expedite rule（轮换发球制）

A rule that comes into play when a game is unfinished at the end of 10 minutes, unless both players have reached 9 points. A point is awarded to the receiver who returns 13 consecutive shots after expedite has been called. Players alternate serves after expedite has been called.

### Five – ball training system（前5板训练法）

A system of training focused on the first five strokes that can occur in every point

### Flip（拧拉短球）

An aggressive topspin return that lands near the net a short ball.

### Footwork（步法）

How a person moves to make a shot.

### Force contact（用力击球）

Contact that results when the racket moves forward when contacting the ball. This type of contact produces forward speed on the ball.

## Forehand（正手）

Any stroke executed with the racket to the right of the elbow for a right – handed player, to the left for a left – handed player.

## Free hand（非持拍手）

The hand not holding the racket.

## Friction contact（摩擦击球）

Contact that results when the racket rushes the ball at contact, imparting spin to the ball.

## Game（局）

The first person to reach 11 points with at least a 2 – point margin wins the game.

## Hard rubber（单胶皮）

A type of racket covering with pips – out rubber but no sponge underneath. It was the most common covering for many years until the development of sponge rubber, but is now rarely used.

## High – toss serve（高抛发球）

A serve in which the ball is thrown high into the air. This increases both spin and deception.

## International Table Tennis FederatIon(ITTF)（国际乒乓球协会）

The inter national governing body for the sport of table tennis.

## Inverted sponge（反胶）

The most common racket covering. It consists of a sheet of pimpled rubber on top of a layer of sponge. The pips point inward, toward the sponge, so the surface is smooth. This is the opposite of pips – out sponge, in which the pips point outward, away from the sponge.

### Kill shot（杀球）

A Stroke executed with maximum speed. See smash.

### Knock – out（淘汰赛）

A competition system of play in which players are eliminated when they lose a single match; also called single elimination.

### Let（干扰球）

A suspension of play for the purpose of replaying the point. A player can call a let when play is interrupted for any reason during a rally.

### Let serve（重发球）

A let that is called when a serve nicks the net. As with other lets, the serve is taken over again. The let serve is the most common type of let.

### Lob（高吊弧圈球）

A high, defensive return of a smash, usually done with topspin or sidespin.

### Loop（弧圈球）

A heavy topspin Shot usually considered the most important shot in the game. Many players specialize in either looping or returning the loop.

### Match（场）

A contest that consists of any odd number of games. Most often a table tennis match consists of either the best three of five games or the best four of seven games.

### Mid – distance aggressive looper（中台弧圈球打法选手）

A player who prefers to play from a few feet（around 1 m）back from the table with strong forehand and backhand topspin strokes.

### Multiball training（多球训练）

A system of practice drills in which a feeder feeds many balls continuously to a person doing a set drill. There is no replay of the ball

### No – spin return（回球不转）

A return with little or no spin.

### Pen – hold grip（直板握法）

A type of grip used mostly by Asian players. It gives the best possible forehand but the most awkward backhand of the conventional grips.

### Pips – out pen – hold style（直板正胶快攻打法选手）

A classic Chinese style of play, featuring strong pen – hold forehand drives and quick backhand blocks.

### Playing surface（台面）

The top of the table, including the edges.

### Power looper（凶狠弧圈球打法选手）

A player who uses a very aggressive style of play based on powerful forehand topspin attacking strokes.

### Punch block（加力推）

A block in which the racket pushes through the ball at contact to add speed.

### Push（搓）

A backspin return of a backspin stroke. The stroke is usually defensive and executed close to or over the table.

### Racket（乒乓球拍）

The implement used to hit the ball; the blade plus the covering.

### Racket hand（持拍手）

The hand that holds the racket.

### Rally（对打）

The hitting of the ball back and forth, commencing with the serve and ending when a point is won.

### Rating（排名数据）

The numerical representation of a players level of play.

### Receive（接球）

The return of a serve.

### Referee（裁判）

The tournament official in charge; the one responsible for ensuring that the event is run according to the rules and for settling any rule disputes.

### Robot（发球机）

A ball – throwing machine that allows a player to practice without a partner.

### Round robin（循环赛）

A competition format in which players are put in small groups in which all players play each other.

### Rubber（胶皮）

The racket covering, sometimes refors only to the rubber on top of a sponge base.

### Rubber cleaner（海绵擦）

A product used to keep the surface inverted rubber clean.

### Sandwich rubber（反胶套胶）

A sponge base covered by a sheet rubber with pips that point either in or out. If the pips point in, it is an inverted sponge. If the pips point out, it is a pips – out sponge.

### Serve（发球）

The first stroke in each point. The server tosses the ball from the palm of the hand and strikes it with the racket as it comes down.

### Shake – hands grip（横版握法）

The most popular grip. It gives the best balance of forehand and backhand strokes.

### Short – pips rubber（正胶）

A type of racket covering that consists of a sheet of pips – out rubber on top of a layer of sponge. The pips point outward, the opposite of inverted. Also called pips – out rubber.

### Sidespin（侧旋）

A type of spin in which the ball spins from left to right or right to left as it moves forward. This is used most often in conjunction with either topspin or backspin.

### Sidespin block（侧切）

A block with sidespin added at contact.

### Smash（扣杀）

A ball that is hit with enough speed to prevent the opponent from making a return：also called a kill shot or a put – away shot.

### Speed glue（快干胶水）

A type of glue that can be put under a sheet of table tennis sponge to make it faster and create more spin. This is now illegal under ITTF and USATT rules.

### Spin（旋转）

The rotation of the ball.

### Sponge（海绵）

The bouncy rubber material used in sandwich covering under a sheet of rubber with pips. It revolutionized the game and ended the hard rubber age of the 1950s.

### Stroke（击球）

Any shot used in the game, including the serve.

### Timing（击球时机）

The ability to choose the point of contact with the ball that will produce the desired stroke.

### Topspin（上旋）

The type of spin produced when the racket brushes the ball while it is moving upward. A ball with topspin spins away from the player after contact.

### Topspin block（带上旋）

A block with added topspin.

### Topspin stroke（loop）（拉球）

An attacking stroke in which the racket contacts the ball while moving from low to high to produce topspin, Heavy topspin strokes are often referred to as loops.

### Umpire（副裁判）

The official who keeps score and enforces rules during a match.

### Underspin（下旋）

See backspin.

### USA Table Tennis（USAT）（美国乒乓球协会）

The governing body of the sport of table tennis in the United States.

# 参考文献
## （Reference）

［1］刘建和.乒乓球教学与训练［M］.北京：人民体育出版社，2011.

［2］苏丕仁. 现代乒乓球运动教学与训练［M］.北京：人民体育出版社，2003.

［3］Richard McAfee. Table Tennis Steps to Success. U. S：Human Kinetics, 2009.

［4］王吉生.乒乓球拍探秘［M］.北京：人民体育出版社，2005.

［5］蔡继玲，吴修文，等.乒乓球［M］.北京：北京体育大学出版社，1999.

［6］魏中明.汉英体育词汇大全［M］.北京：人民体育出版社，1999.

［7］中国乒乓球协会.乒乓球竞赛规则［M］.北京：人民体育出版社，2003.

［8］全国体育院校教材委员会审定.乒乓球［M］.北京：人民体育出版社，2003.

［9］Dan Seemiller. Winning Table Tennis. U. S：Human Kinetics, 1997.

［10］李秉德.教学论［M］.北京：人们教育出版社，2000.

［11］侯文达.高等学校乒乓球教材——教学与训练［M］.北京：北京大学出版社，1994.

［12］体育院系教材编审委员会.乒乓球［M］.北京：人民体育出版社，1979.

［13］岑淮光等.怎么打好乒乓球［M］.北京：人民体育出版社，2001.

［14］温国昌.乒乓球教学与训练［M］.郑州：河南科学技术出版社，1986.

［15］凌群立，等.教你打乒乓球［M］.南京：江苏科学技术出版社，1999.

［16］王道俊、王汉澜，等.教育学［M］.北京：人民教育出版社，1989.

［17］全国体育院校教材委员会审定.运动训练学［M］.北京：人民体育出版社，2000.

［18］邱钟惠，等.现代乒乓球技术的研究［M］.北京：人民体育出版社，1982.

［19］郝光安，等.网球、羽毛球、乒乓球技法入门［M］.北京：北京体育大学出版社，1994.

［20］滕守刚.乒乓球高手［M］.长沙：湖南文艺出版社，1999.

［21］赵修琴.中国乒乓球图解技战术全书［M］.北京：中国物资出版社，1999.

［22］程云峰.图解乒乓球基础技术［M］.哈尔滨：黑龙江科学技术出版社，1998.

［23］林晓彦.乒乓球入门［M］.合肥：安徽科学技术出版社，1998.

［24］程嘉炎.球类运动竞赛法［M］.北京：人民体育出版社，2003.

［25］岳海鹏.乒乓球打法与战术［M］.北京：人民体育出版社，2002.

［26］谢亚龙，王汝英等.中国优秀项目制规律［M］.北京：人民体育出版社，1992.

［27］谭朕斌.篮球技术教学与训练［M］.北京：北京体育大学出版社，2010.

**图书在版编目(CIP)数据**

乒乓球汉英双语教程 / 何阳编著. —2 版. —长沙：
中南大学出版社，2021.1(2021.12 重印)
　　ISBN 978-7-5487-3383-6

　　Ⅰ.①乒… Ⅱ.①何… Ⅲ.①乒乓球运动—双语教学
—高等学校—教材—汉、英 Ⅳ.①G846

中国版本图书馆 CIP 数据核字(2018)第 202339 号

**乒乓球汉英双语教程(第二版)**
PINGPANGQIU HANYING SHUANGYU JIAOCHENG（DI-ER BAN)

何阳　编著

□**责任编辑**　汪采知
□**责任印制**　唐　曦
□**出版发行**　中南大学出版社
　　　　　　　社址：长沙市麓山南路　　　邮编：410083
　　　　　　　发行科电话：0731-88876770　传真：0731-88710482
□**印　　装**　湖南省汇昌印务有限公司

□**开　本**　710 mm×1000 mm 1/16　□**印张** 12.25　□**字数** 310 千字
□**版　次**　2021 年 1 月第 2 版　□**印次** 2021 年 12 月第 2 次印刷
□**书　号**　ISBN 978-7-5487-3383-6
□**定　价**　36.00 元

图书出现印装问题，请与经销商调换